PICTURE LETTERS
FROM THE
COMMANDER IN CHIEF

By Tadamichi Kuribayashi
Edited by Tsuyuko Yoshida

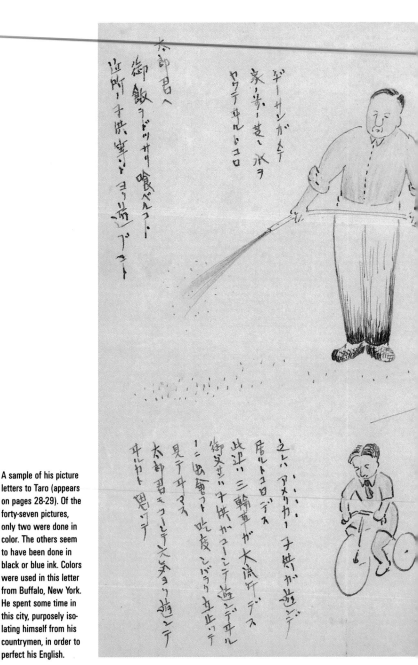

太郎君へ

御飯ヲドッサリ喰ベテ……
近所ノ子供等ト ヨク遊ンデマース

ヂーサンガ出テ
家ノ前ニ蒔ク水ヲ
ヤッテ居ルトコロ

立ハ、アメリカノ子供ガ遊デ
居ルトコロデス
此辺ハ三輪車ガ大流行デス
御父サンハ子供ガ コーシテ遊ンデ居ル
ニ出會フト 吃度 ニッコリ立止ッテ
見テ井マス
太郎君モ コーシテ大キョリ遊ンデ
井ルカト思ッテ

A sample of his picture letters to Taro (appears on pages 28-29). Of the forty-seven pictures, only two were done in color. The others seem to have been done in black or blue ink. Colors were used in this letter from Buffalo, New York. He spent some time in this city, purposely isolating himself from his countrymen, in order to perfect his English.

太郎君へ
父より

コハ御父サンガ今居ルバツフアローノセームスヂス
此附近(帝ノ住居ヲ)通ッテ居ル一番ニギヤカナ
人通リデ皆此ブラシブダツニナツテ居ル大変キレ
イナ所デス(左ノ方ニアルノハ御父サンガ毎ロ
出カケルワウィツフトイフ所ノ大学ノ前デス)ケレ

下ノ方ニ
居ルノ
ハ人
デス

Another drawing of a boulevard in Buffalo, using color (pages 32-33).

At right: A photograph of Taro which Kuribayashi took to the U.S. and supposedly carried with him everywhere he went. At that time, Taro was his only child. Above: A photograph of Takako, taken in August 1943 with relatives. Ten months later, Tadamichi started to write letters to Takako from the battlefield.

昭和　年　月　日

たこちゃんへ

たこちゃん（月六日の手紙は前よりよく書けておりましたね

そして知って居やうとは思はなかった 難しい文句を沢山

使ってねるのには がっくりとしましたよ、浩躍とか、鬼畜とか

攻撃精神が、撃滅せんとか、銃後とか……

しかしほんとう意味がよく判って居るものがゐね 含ってあるのかしら

お父さんが気が付かない間にずい分 利口になったもので

お父さんも嬉しく思ます

手紙の字は次の立ったサ間違ってゐました。

鬼畜（鬼畜）、攻め寄せて（攻め寄せて）

撃滅（撃滅）空襲（空襲）身体（身体）

次にお父さんの方も朝晩は少し寒くなりましたがまだ

夏服で居ります 草や木も青々としておなし蝿も

栗林忠道

字へ ←

The last letter that Kuribayashi wrote from Iwo Jima was on headed notepaper, and filled both sides. He was a keen educator and even corrected errors in Takako's letters. Expressions reflect wartime sentiment.

Kuribayashi with his automobile, the Chevrolet K. He enjoyed touring the countryside and discovering America firsthand.

This photograph was taken in 1931 at the Japanese Legation in Canada, when he was appointed First Military Attaché. Kuribayashi is shown in the back row, second from the right.

Kuribayashi commanding his men. He carried a slender walking stick and is said to have walked all over the island.

Lieutenant General Kuribayashi was promoted to full General after his honorable death on Iwo Jima.

Kuribayashi's (center) wise leadership won the praise of even his enemies during the struggle between American and Japanese troops.

The U.S. Army lay siege to Mount Suribachi, where a Japanese battery was ensconced (The photos above and below courtesy of U.S. Marine Corps).

The operation projected to take five days actually lasted thirty-five days. About 20,000 Japanese soldiers died.

PICTURE LETTERS
FROM THE
COMMANDER IN CHIEF

By TADAMICHI KURIBAYASHI
EDITED BY TSUYUKO YOSHIDA

VIZ Media

San Francisco

Picture Letters from the Commander in Chief

By Tadamichi Kuribayashi
Edited by Tsuyuko Yoshida

Translation/Michi Fusayama
Design/Izumi Evers & Sam Elzway

Published by
VIZ Media, LLC
295 Bay St.
San Francisco, CA 94133

www.viz.com

Library of Congress Cataloging-in-Publication Data

Kuribayashi, Tadamichi, 1890 or 1-1945.
["Gyokusai Soshikikan" no etegami. English]
Picture Letters from the Commander in Chief / by Tadamichi
Kuribayashi ; edited by Tsuyuko Yoshida.
p. cm.
Includes bibliographical references and index.
ISBN-13: 978-1-4215-1845-9 (pbk. : alk. paper)
ISBN-10: 1-4215-1845-7 (pbk. : alk. paper)
1. Kuribayashi, Tadamichi, 1890 or 1-1945–Correspondence.
2. Japan. Rikugun–Officers–Correspondence. 3. Iwo Jima, Battle of, Japan, 1945.
I. Yoshida, Tsuyuko. II. Title.
DS890.K77613A4 2007
940.54'2528092–dc22

                                                    2007014698

Printed in the U.S.A.

First printing, June 2007

Contents

Foreword by Clint Eastwood..4

Editor's notes..6

To Taro From March 1928 to April 1930..7

Kuribayashi's travels across the U.S...8

Commentary

    Regarding army officers and their studies abroad...15

    Ranks, branches and organization within the Japanese army.............................27

    Practical English..39

    Young Kuribayashi and his dreams..59

    America—a hypothetical enemy..67

    America in the latter half of the 1920s..79

    Horses and a Chevrolet...95

    Ft. Bliss and Ft. Riley..105

    A German shepherd named Marie...111

    "The Marching Song for Horses"...127

    Military attaché at the Japanese Legation in Canada.......................................153

    Kazunoko and Johnny Walker Red...179

    About Tadamichi Kuribayashi's family...201

To Tako-chan From June 1944 to January 1945 (from Iwo Jima).....................................215

Commentary

    How the illustrated letters came to be released..226

To my wife and children From June 25, 1944 to February 3, 1945 (from Iwo Jima).............227

Farewell wire from Commander Kuribayashi, 24:00 hours, March 17, 1945.....................233

Battle of Iwo Jima by Shigetoki Hosoki..234

Commentary by Koichi Edagawa...239

Chronology of the life and times of Tadamichi Kuribayashi..244

Afterword by Iris Yamashita...252

Clint Eastwood (director)

An interest in the battle of Iwo Jima and the many lives lost there led me to discover the fascinating story of General Tadamichi Kuribayashi. His letters to his wife and children reveal a man of profound sincerity and kindness. Through gentle reminders to a son to care for his mother and a heartfelt farewell to his wife, the letters complete the picture of the legendary military strategist.

It was these letters that compelled me to think about the lives of all the Japanese soldiers who bravely fought and died on that island. I was proud to have the opportunity to bring their story to the screen for today's generation. *Letters from Iwo Jima* is my tribute to the forgotten men of that battle and the countless others of World War II.

Sincerely,
Clint Eastwood

(left to right) Interpreter Yuki Ishimaru, director Clint Eastwood, and Ken Watanabe as General Kuribayashi on the set of Warner Bros. Pictures and DreamWorks Pictures' World War II drama *Letters from Iwo Jima*, directed by Clint Eastwood.

Editor's notes

This book is a compilation of illustrated letters from Tadamichi
Kurabayashi. The letters were sent to his eldest son Taro from
America between 1928 and 1931; forty-seven illustrations (forty-two
sheets, five of which were illustrated on both sides) were saved and
included in this book. Also included in this book are letters sent
from Kurabayashi between 1944 and 1945 from Iwo Jima; seven are
addressed to his daughter Takako, and two addressed to his wife,
Yoshii, and the children.

The envelopes for these letters no longer exist. There are also mis-
sives that do not state the date or location from which they were
written. It is presumed that many of the letters may have been
mailed in a bundle. The illustrations in this book are arranged in
chronological order, and in many cases, the editor inferred the date of
illustration from the location and scenario depicted.

The letters from Iwo Jima are all dated and are arranged in chronological order.

TO TARO

From March 1928 to April 1930

Studying military
affairs in America,
Army Cavalry
Captain Tadamichi
Kuribayashi (thirty-
eight years old) wrote
to his eldest son Taro
(three years old).
Because Taro was too
young to read kanji
(characters), the
father illustrated the
letters and asked his
wife Yoshii to read
them to their son.

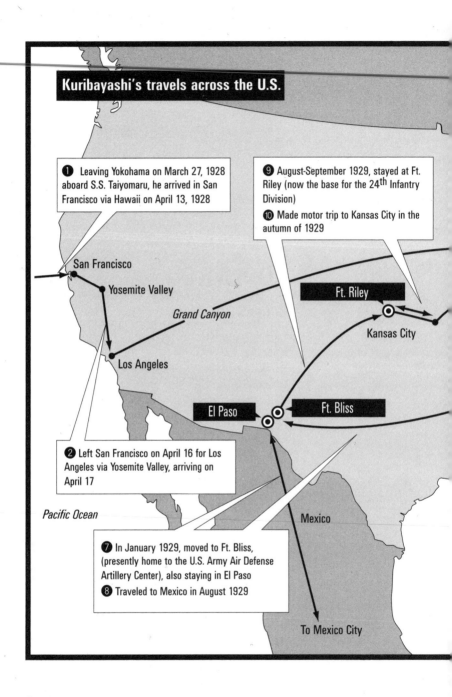

Kuribayashi's travels across the U.S.

① Leaving Yokohama on March 27, 1928 aboard S.S. Taiyomaru, he arrived in San Francisco via Hawaii on April 13, 1928

⑨ August-September 1929, stayed at Ft. Riley (now the base for the 24th Infantry Division)

⑩ Made motor trip to Kansas City in the autumn of 1929

San Francisco

Yosemite Valley

Grand Canyon

Ft. Riley

Kansas City

Los Angeles

El Paso

Ft. Bliss

② Left San Francisco on April 16 for Los Angeles via Yosemite Valley, arriving on April 17

Pacific Ocean

Mexico

⑦ In January 1929, moved to Ft. Bliss, (presently home to the U.S. Army Air Defense Artillery Center), also staying in El Paso

⑧ Traveled to Mexico in August 1929

To Mexico City

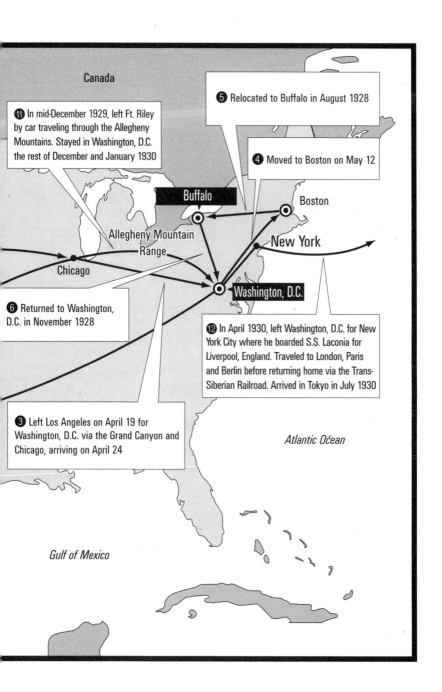

Canada

⑤ Relocated to Buffalo in August 1928

⑪ In mid-December 1929, left Ft. Riley by car traveling through the Allegheny Mountains. Stayed in Washington, D.C. the rest of December and January 1930

④ Moved to Boston on May 12

Buffalo

Boston

Allegheny Mountain Range

New York

Chicago

Washington, D.C.

⑥ Returned to Washington, D.C. in November 1928

⑫ In April 1930, left Washington, D.C. for New York City where he boarded S.S. Laconia for Liverpool, England. Traveled to London, Paris and Berlin before returning home via the Trans-Siberian Railroad. Arrived in Tokyo in July 1930

③ Left Los Angeles on April 19 for Washington, D.C. via the Grand Canyon and Chicago, arriving on April 24

Atlantic Ocean

Gulf of Mexico

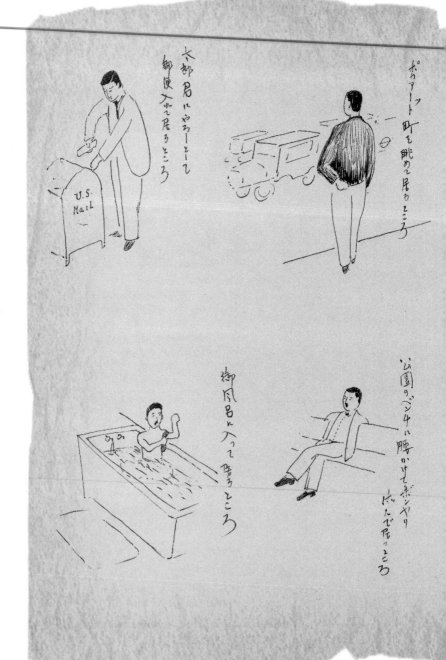

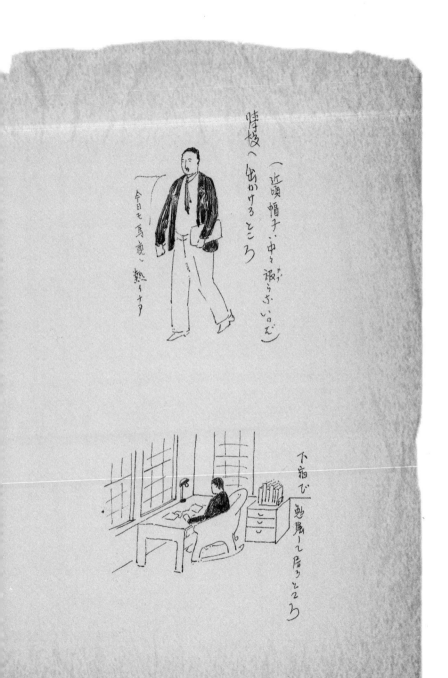

下宿で 勉強して居るところ

上接へ 出かけるところ

（近頃帽子、中々被らないので）

今日モ馬鹿ニ熱イナア

A DAY IN MY LIFE

The heat is oppressive today.

(I often go without a hat these days.)
Leaving for school.

Studying in my room at the boarding house.

Gazing vacantly
at the cityscape.

Idly resting on a
park bench.

A DAY IN MY LIFE

Posting my letter to Taro.

Taking a bath.

Regarding army officers and their studies abroad

It was common practice to encourage Army University honor students to continue their education abroad. A total of twenty-eight graduates were sent overseas during a three-year period following Kuribayashi's graduation. Ten alumni were sent to Germany, seven to France, one to England, four to America, one to Poland, two to the USSR, and three to China.

The Japanese army, it should be remembered, was modeled in 1886 after its counterpart in Germany. Perhaps this explains the small number of students sent to England and the U.S. Looking back, such a bias may have played a role in Japan's subsequent defeat in the war.

On the eve of his departure, Kuribayashi hosted a party for sixty guests (see page 174). The affair cost him ¥600 (roughly $300). Saburo Endo, a classmate of Kuribayashi who was on his way to France, happened to keep detailed notes. The monthly stipend for a student at that time was ¥500 (which was equal to a general's salary). Endo recalls: "It was more than enough. I often entertained friends, diplomats among them." Endo received ¥1,875 to cover travel expenses when he left Japan. With the twenty percent discount extended for official travel, he paid ¥788.97 for the voyage from Yokohama to Marseilles.

But when Major Endo returned home, his monthly salary shriveled to ¥190. "I handed my wife ¥160 for household expenses, which left me with a mere ¥30 for spending money," he said. An ordinance in 1931 authorized a ten percent cut in government salaries. With the onslaught of a global depression, the army's coffers were depleted.

屋

— To Taro —

THE VIEW TO THE NORTH: July 20

北ノ窓ノ眺望
ハーバード大學北郊ノ住宅地ヲ俯瞰ス
遠ク遙ニ霞メルハサンヌービル
右ノ高塔ハ博物館ノ時計台
直ク眼下ニアルハ他ノビルデングノ屋上、納涼ノ
美人時々徘徊ス
東ノ窓ヨリハボストンヲ望ム、眺望殆ト之ニ
似タリ

THE VIEW TO THE NORTH

There is a residential area to the north of
Harvard University, and in the distance you can
see Somerville in the mist. The structure on the
left is the museum clock tower, and directly
under my window are rooftops of various other
buildings. At times, pretty ladies stroll along
the streets to escape the heat.

The city of Boston can be seen to the east. The
rest of the views are similar.

THE CATS HERE ARE THE SAME AS IN JAPAN:
To Taro, from Father

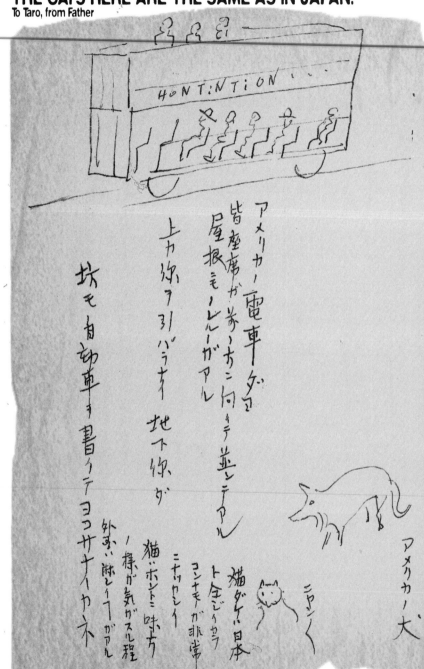

太郎君へ　父ヨリ

道ヲ横切ルニハ御気ヲ
何時モ〱非常ニ注意
又ネバラナイ
りしい澤山ケキ交ヒレテルセフダ

澤山アリマス

アメリカニハ自動車ガ

21

I have to be very careful when crossing the street.
Cars come from every direction.

America is filled with cars.

Here's an American train. All the seats face forward. If you want, you can sit on the roofs of some of them.

There are no overhead wires; the lines are underground.

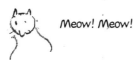

Meow! Meow!

An American dog.

Cats are the only thing America has in common with Japan. I feel very close to them. At times they seem like my only friends. I yearn for home.

Why don't you draw a car for me, Taro?

LYING DOWN IN HARVARD: To show Taro how Father is faring
(drawing done on August 18)

太郎君ニ　智さん　御安心ノ様子

八月十八日　描ク

余り暑いから
ハーバード大学ノ庭
ヘ行テ寝ソベツテ
居るところ

リスが
来る

LYING DOWN IN HARVARD: To show Taro how Father is faring
(drawing done on August 18)

It is very hot. I went to the grounds of Harvard University to lie down.

A squirrel visits.

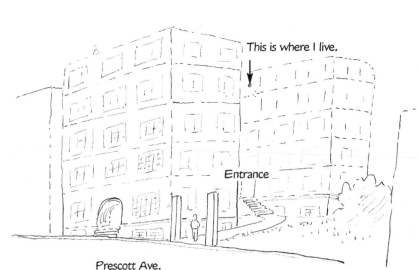

This is where I live.

Entrance

Prescott Ave.

Ranks, branches and organization within the Japanese army

A soldier is a member of a branch and an organization, and is assigned a rank. His rank corresponds to his position in the organization. For instance, in 1923 Kuribayashi was Cavalry Captain (rank and branch), and his position was Company Commander in the 15th Cavalry Regiment (organization). The largest unit in the organization is the division. The Guards Division and the First Division were both located in Tokyo. By the end of the Meiji era, there were fifteen divisions, and that number increased with each new year.

Kuribayashi finished middle school (under the old system) when he was twenty years old and enrolled in the Army Officers Academy. There, he was made Second Lieutenant and went on to study for a year at the Cavalry Academy. He was promoted to Lieutenant and entered the Army University where he did the equivalent of post-graduate work.

Kuribayashi graduated from the Army University at the age of thirty-three. He was an elite member of the army.

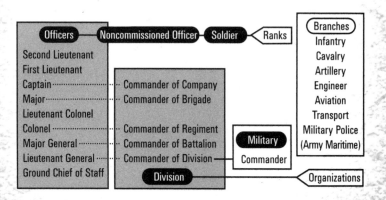

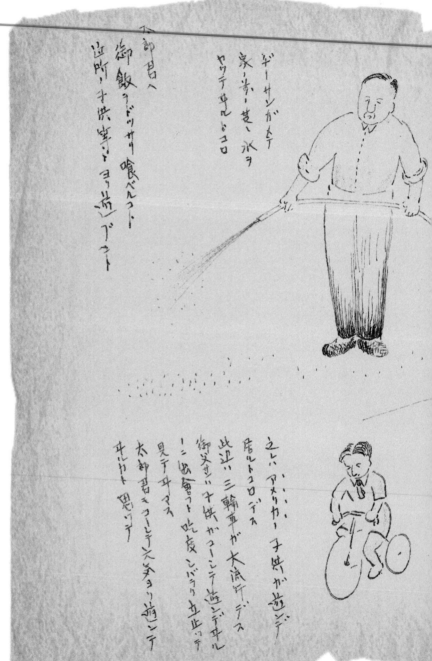

太郎君へ

御飯ヲドッサリ喰ベルコト
近所ノ子供等ニョリ遊バスコト

ギーサンガ来テ
家ノ前ノ芝ニ水ヲ
ヤッテヰルトコロ

立ヘ、、、、、、アメリカノ子供ガ遊ンデ
居ルトコロデス
此辺ハ三輪車ガ大流行デス
御父サンハ子供ガコーシテ遊ンデヰル
ニ必會フト吃度ノバラク立止ッテ
見テヰマス
太郎君ヤコーシテ大ショリ遊ンデ
井ルカト思ッテ

御父サンハ今ソレヲ見ナガラ
ダーサンニ日本ノ話ヲシテ
キカセテ居ルトコロ

一九日木曜日

日本語デ
「ソレ行ケノく」

バツファロージヨリ

太郎君ヘ

TRICYCLE BOOM: -- 27, to Taro, from Father in Buffalo, New York

The old man is watering his lawn.

Here are some American children at play. Tricycles are very popular around here. Whenever I see kids playing, I stop to watch and wonder if Taro is happily playing at home.

I stop to chat,
telling him all about
Japan.

In Japan, they would be shouting "sore-ike,
sore-ike!" [Go, go!]

Taro, be sure to eat well and play
nicely with your friends.

太郎君へ

九月十五日、

ヨーハ　御父サンが　今居ル、バッファロ、　セントゼームス「通」デス

此附近、一帯ノ住宅地デ　通モ広ク区域ガ皆此ノ通リデアッテ

入ル通リモ余リナク大変静カデス（十五分デ行カレル下町ニ行クト

ゴッタ返シ！ニギヤカナリ）

子供が
遊ンデ
居ル

THIS IS ST. JAMES STREET: September 15, to Taro

This is St. James Street in Buffalo, where I now live. It is a residential neighborhood, and as you can see, it is very big. There are very few people on the streets and it is very quiet.

(A fifteen-minute drive will take you to the crowds and noise downtown.)

Children at play.

今ヤ窓ノ外ハ冬ノ仕度ニ
色々何ヤラ漬カ其ノ下
毎日働キ通シ
デス

八月十九日 寓ス

太郎君へ

之ハアメリカノ御菓子達が

御勝手デ　べらくヽシャベリトウ

働キ子屋ルトコロデス

靑ヽ着物ノ不着ノ

涼サンデス

桃ノ皮タムイテ産ルノ三階

二居ル御遂式サンデ　手ヲ傳フ

ホタノデス

日本デ御菜漬ヲ漬ケル様ニ

バツフアローノ父ヨリ

This drawing shows some elderly American women chatting up a storm as they work in the kitchen.

The one in blue is my landlady.

The one peeling a peach lives on the third floor. She has come down to help.

Much like how Japanese women pickle vegetables, my landlady makes preserves to store for the winter. She works all day.

Practical English

In a letter to his brother, Kuribayashi wrote that he was "taken aback by the barrage of English from the hawkers" who met him as he disembarked in San Francisco on April 14, 1928. He went on to say that his consternation could "be attributed to my lack of training in practical English." English was Kuribayashi's forte in middle school, but conversational English was difficult for him.

Kuribayashi spent some time in Buffalo, a medium-sized city in New York near Niagara Falls. He took time off from his studies at Harvard University, after his visit to Washington, D.C. August of 1928 found him boarding with a local family in Buffalo. His intention was to reside in a city where there was no Japanese population to speak of, and polish up his conversational English. All military officers sent abroad to study had to undergo this demanding course of study.

Apparently, it brought results. Writing from Ft. Bliss, Texas in 1928, Kuribayashi said that he was able to hold lively conversations with his friend Captain Weitman and his family (page 80).

Taro Kuribayashi, who grew up to become an architect, once remarked that he was "surprised at my father's familiarity with architectural terminology in English." Among the English books that sit in the Kuribayashi family library is a thick volume about the actor Gary Cooper.

But the best by-product of his stay in America had to be his deepened understanding of his host country. Hirohide Iwasaki, who once worked under Kuribayashi, recalls that even when Japan was gaining ground in the war circa 1941, Kuribayashi cautioned, "Japan should not underestimate America."

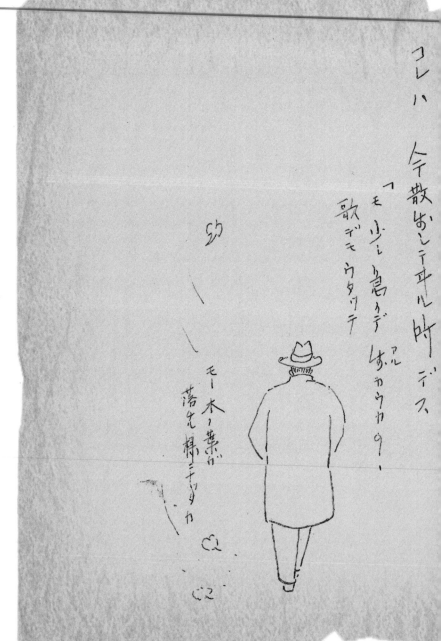

太郎君へ

坊達ノ寫真ヲ
見テヰル所。

イヤー！
水キリオッタナ！
エヽイ、
三輪車ガ
ハヽ文ノ御友達ヨ。、
何ンダ 何テ小サナ赤ンボダ

有介 バッファロノ
父ヨリ

41

I am gazing at photos of you and the others.
"Goodness, how you have grown!"
"This is a fine tricycle."
"Well now, is this a friend of yours?"
"My! What a tiny baby."

Here I am taking a walk.
"Should I step it up? And sing a song."
The leaves have started to fall.

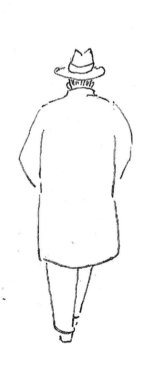

太郎君へ

御父サンハ寒クテモ かまハズ
運動ヲシテオルカラ 大変
大夫デス、

十月 ―
バッ夛ロ三 父

御母サンハ 御父サンニ画ヲカク事ヲ近
心配シテヨコスガ 太郎君ハ画ガ
ナイト御父サンノ様子ガ ちがウ ワケ
コレニ此ト 画ヲカウニハ 御母サンノ
心配スル程 熱中シモノデモナイ
言ッテ 一筆書キヤンダ

大ク降ッテ来タナ
此ゲダト 積ルカモ 知レナイ‥‥‥
少シ手ヲ振ッテ ちゃウカ
運動トハ 様ニ‥‥‥
手袋ヲ持ッテ来ジバ 己ガウタナ

45

EXERCISING IN THE COLD: October --, to Taro,
from Father in Buffalo, New York

I keep fit by exercising regularly, even in cold weather.

Your mother worries about my constant drawing.
But Taro would not understand [my letters] without them.
Also, my drawings do not require as much attention as your mother imagines.
They are just sketches.

The snow is falling heavily. Perhaps it will pile up…
I'd better swing my arms as I walk, for the exercise…
I should have brought along my gloves…
Here is the boy next door calling out to me while I study.
He is a funny, lively boy called "White."

Here is the father of the junior high
school student next door.
He's yelling to your father who's
studying.
He's a funny kid with a lot of energy.
The boy's name is "White."

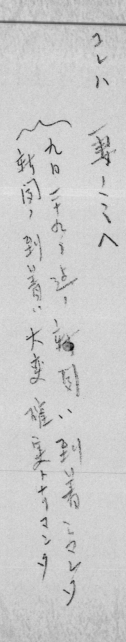

タロヘ

〔九日二十九ニ達シ、新聞、到着、大変確定ヲナシマシタ
新聞、到着、到着ニ〇〇レリ〕

Message to my wife:
The newspapers [you sent] through
September 27 have arrived.
The newspapers are arriving more regularly.

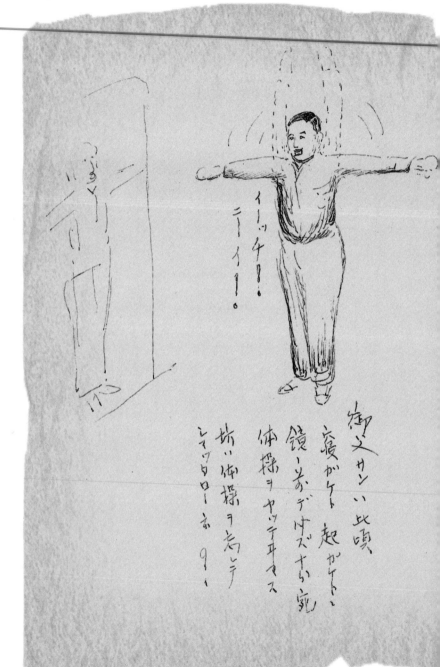

イーッチ！
テーイ！。

御父サンハ此頃、
寝ガケト　起ガケニ、
鏡ノ前デサウシテ寛
体操ヲヤッテヰマス
坊ハ体操ヲ為シテ
ヰマスカ　タロー　ネ。

太郎君へ

ナツカシイノ
パッパヤ 市父ヨリ

下病ノ御バーサンガボーノ子供ノ
パッツェートト云フ四才ニナル子ガ
御父サンニ 邪魔ニ来テ
十日許リ来テ泊リ始終
家ニ居ルト 御父サンハサンーヲ六方ヘヤリ
～ニファ・デ・バーサンデ 連レテ来タルデス
成程 イタヅラデムヤミニ 困カサレテ
人慣レショリテ 御父サンモ遊々
持テ来シテンマツタガ 一昨日ホント
ー家ヘ ツレテ行カレマシタ

ミスター クルバーシン
ドウ ユー ライク ミーヤ、
ヴェー マ、4ヤ、
ザン ダーローヤ、
（太郎君ー名ヲ知ッテ居ルデス）

Patsy is my elderly landlady's four-year-old niece. She has come to stay for ten days and constantly comes to my room. Her mother has her hands full and so the landlady has brought her here. She is mischievous, friendly and a handful. She was always in my hair, but she left for home yesterday.

"Mr. Kuru-ba-shi, do you like me? Very much? (More) than Taarou?"
(Yes, Taro, she knows your name.)

I routinely exercise for ten minutes in front of the
mirror before bed and after I wake.
I bet you've forgotten how to exercise.

One! Two!

アメリカノ電車.

ケムリヲポツポツ出シテ

走ルイ 中デ ダンロヲ焚イテ

居ルカラウデス

電車ノ やねノ上ニ 坊ノ好キナ

カラクリガ 無イノハ

電車道ノ 眞中ニ 掘リ深イ

溝ニ 引 軌條ガ アツテ 其代用

ヲレテ 居ルカラウデ アリマス

「バツフアロ」

下宿ノ下婆サンヤ

近所ノ片バサン達ガ

皆キニテ 此父サンガ

帰テシマウノヲ惜シガツテ

居ルトコロ デス

此父サンハ サン程 皆サ?

好カレマシタ

TAX
タキシー

ブーブー

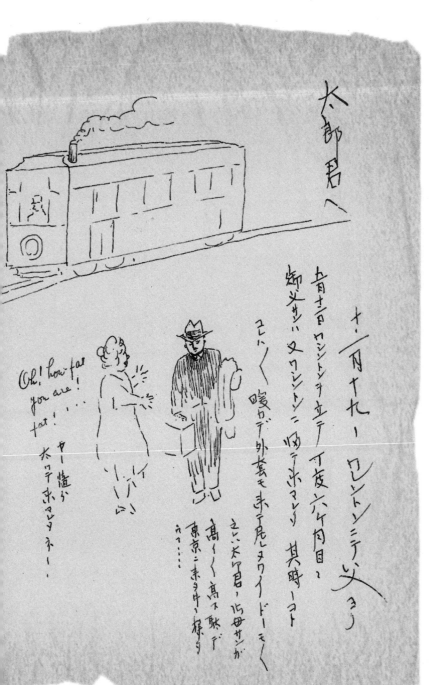

BACK IN WASHINGTON: November 19, to Taro, from Father in Washington, D.C.

Here is an American train. Smoke billows out now and again because a stove is kept burning inside the train.

There are no bars on the roof (unlike the ones you're familiar with).

Instead they have a narrow grooved rail running in the middle of the tracks.

Oh, How
fat you are!
Fat!

I left Washington on May 12 and have returned exactly six
months later.
It's so warm here, I have taken off my overcoat.
It reminds me of your mother when she came to Tokyo
wearing her high wooden clogs. Haha...

— To Taro —

BACK IN WASHINGTON: November 19, to Taro, from Father in Washington, D.C.

Here is my elderly landlady and some neighbors bidding me goodbye. They say they will miss me.
We have become good friends.

TAX
タキ：ー

Honk!
Honk!

Young Kuribayashi and his dreams

Tadamichi Kuribayashi was born on July 7, 1891, in Nagano
Prefecture (presently known as Saijo, Matsushiro-machi, Nagano
City). He was the second son of Tsurujiro and Moto Kuribayashi,
and his family were proud of their samurai lineage. After finishing
elementary school, Tadamichi was enrolled at Nagano Middle
School. His older brother, Yoshima, excelled in school but chose
to work on the family farm rather than pursue higher education.
Tadamichi, however, pressed onward with his education.
Encouraged by a friend, Kuribayashi took an interest in English
and read *Hamlet* in its original text during his fourth year in
middle school. He also exercised a lot. Exercising and walking
are habits he acquired during his boyhood and appear often in his
illustrated letters.

Kuribayashi dreamed of becoming a journalist or a diplomat, but
his family could not afford to pay for an exclusive education in
English. Therefore, he applied to the Shanghai Toa Dobun Shoin
(an educational institution specializing in languages and business
which trained many future journalists, diplomats and business
executives), and the Army Officers Academy. He was accepted to
both. Influenced in no small way by advice from his elder brother
who had tasted victory in the Russo-Japanese War, Kuribayashi
chose to enroll in the Army Academy.

Kuribayashi selected a military career, but was sent to the U.S. to
study. He ultimately served as a military attaché involved in
diplomatic matters. He did not become a journalist, but as you
will note in his collection of letters, he possessed indispensable
journalistic qualifications, such as the powers of observation and
literary expression. It can be said that having had this collection
of writings published, Kuribayashi's dreams have finally come
true, half a century after his death.

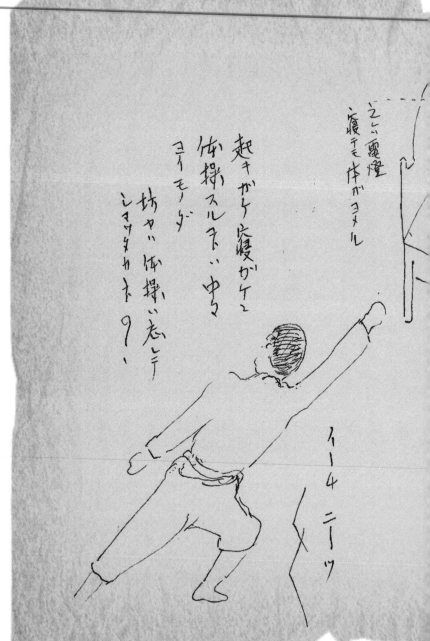

太郎君へ

十二日三〇　ワシントンニテ

父ヨリ

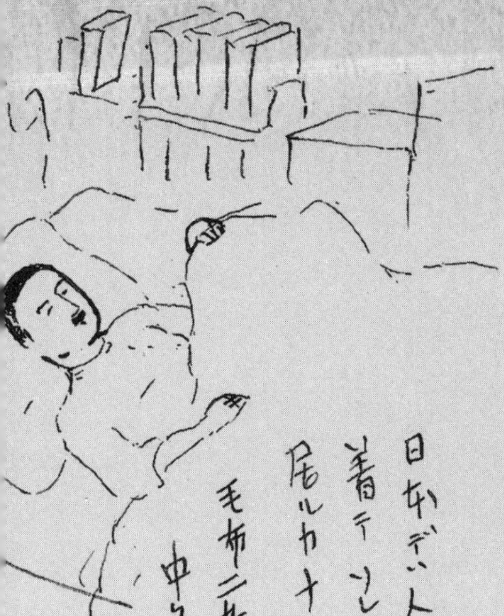

御父サンガ今、寝ンネシテ居ルトコロ

日本デハ今頃、身動キガ出来ヌ程、夜具ヲ着テ、ソレデ、肩ガ、、、レナド、云フテ居ルカナ、、、、ソレニ、コゝデハ

毛布二枚シカ掛ケテ居ナイ〜て
中々　アタイナア
コレマクリテシマウ〜カ

61

SLEEPING AT NIGHT: December 3, to Taro, from Father in Washington, D.C.

Here is my light.
I can read in
bed.

Here is your father sleeping at night.

I imagine that in Japan, you have two heavy quilts over you
and are still complaining that your shoulders are cold.
Here, I only need two blankets and even then, I am hot.
I think I'll take them off.

Exercising before and after sleep is good for you.
Have you forgotten how?

One, two.
One, two.

I AM PACKING AGAIN: December 23, to Taro, from Father in Washington, D.C.

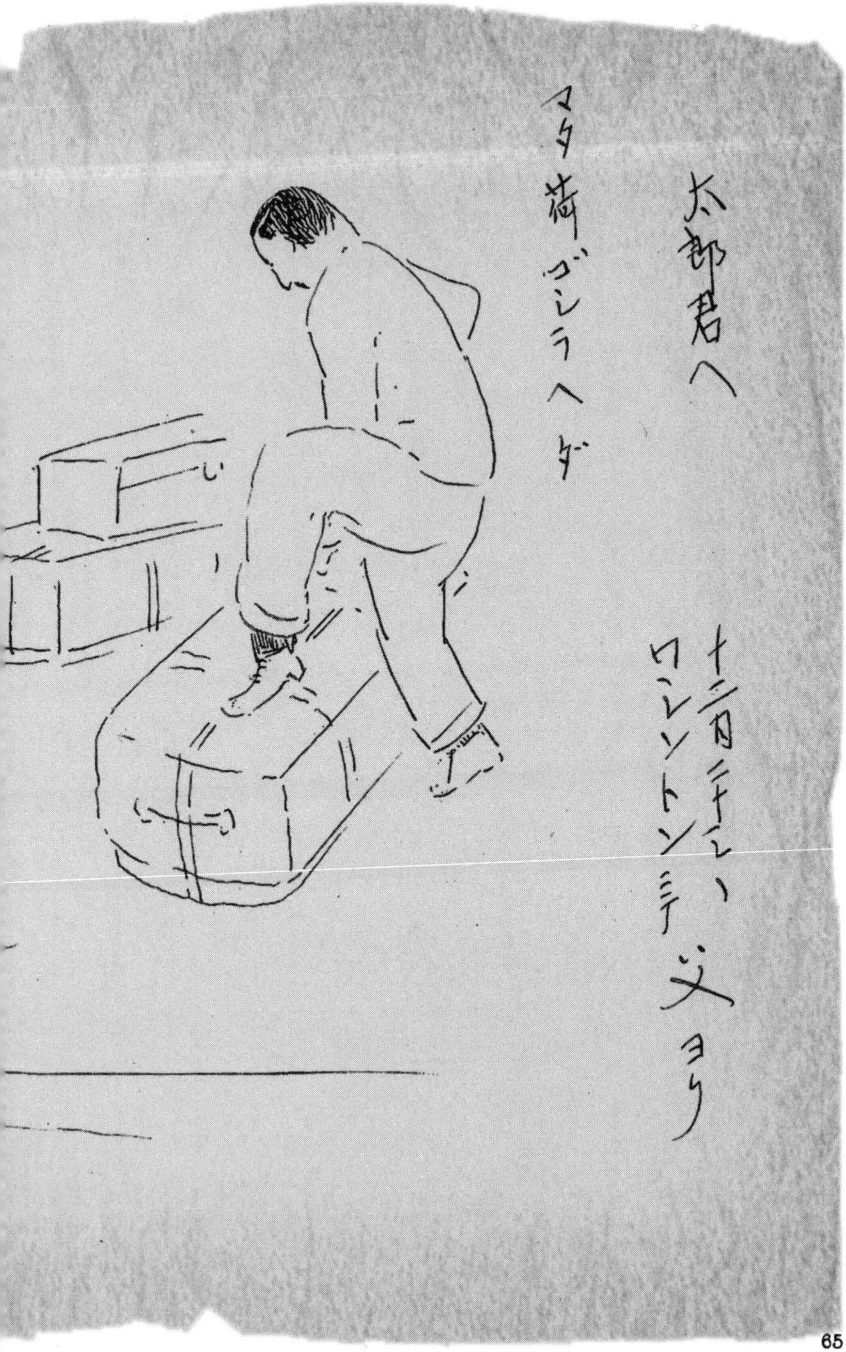

太郎君へ

マタ荷ゴシラヘダ

十二月三十一ハ
ワシントンデ父ヨリ

I am packing my bags again.

To Texas...

America—a hypothetical enemy

A law passed in May 1924 barring Japanese from immigrating to California upset Japan a great deal. It was in September of the same year that the U.S. army began to strengthen its "Plan Orange," which was in essence a war strategy against Japan. For its part, the Japanese army organized a "Committee to Study the Preparation for a War Against America" in 1924, and drew up plans to defeat the American Fleet by attacking the Cavite Naval Yard (thirty kilometers southwest of Manila, in the Philippines). Should the Americans approach, Japan would meet them head on and repeat the victory they savored over the Baltic Fleet in the Russo-Japanese War.

Thus began the confrontation between Japan and America. In a naval conference in London in 1930, Japan insisted on a naval ratio vis-à-vis America of seventy percent. After a tough negotiation period, they finally agreed to 69.7 percent. The Japanese Ambassador at that time was Katsuji Debuchi, who was a special appointee of then-Foreign Minister Kijuro Shidehara. Debuchi was a proponent of Shidehara's "International Cooperation Diplomacy" and enjoyed the trust of his American counterparts.

Col. Hisao Watari, the Japanese military attaché in Washington at the time, was Kuribayashi's superior. Watari reported to the Minister of the Army, Kazushige Ugaki, that the possibility of America becoming an enemy of Japan was very limited. "If the Japanese Empire plans the development of China according to the laws stipulated under the equal opportunity policy, there is little chance that America will go to war with Japan."

Under such circumstances, America was indeed a hypothetical enemy as far as Japan was concerned. Kuribayashi was thus able to enjoy life in America undeterred by politics.

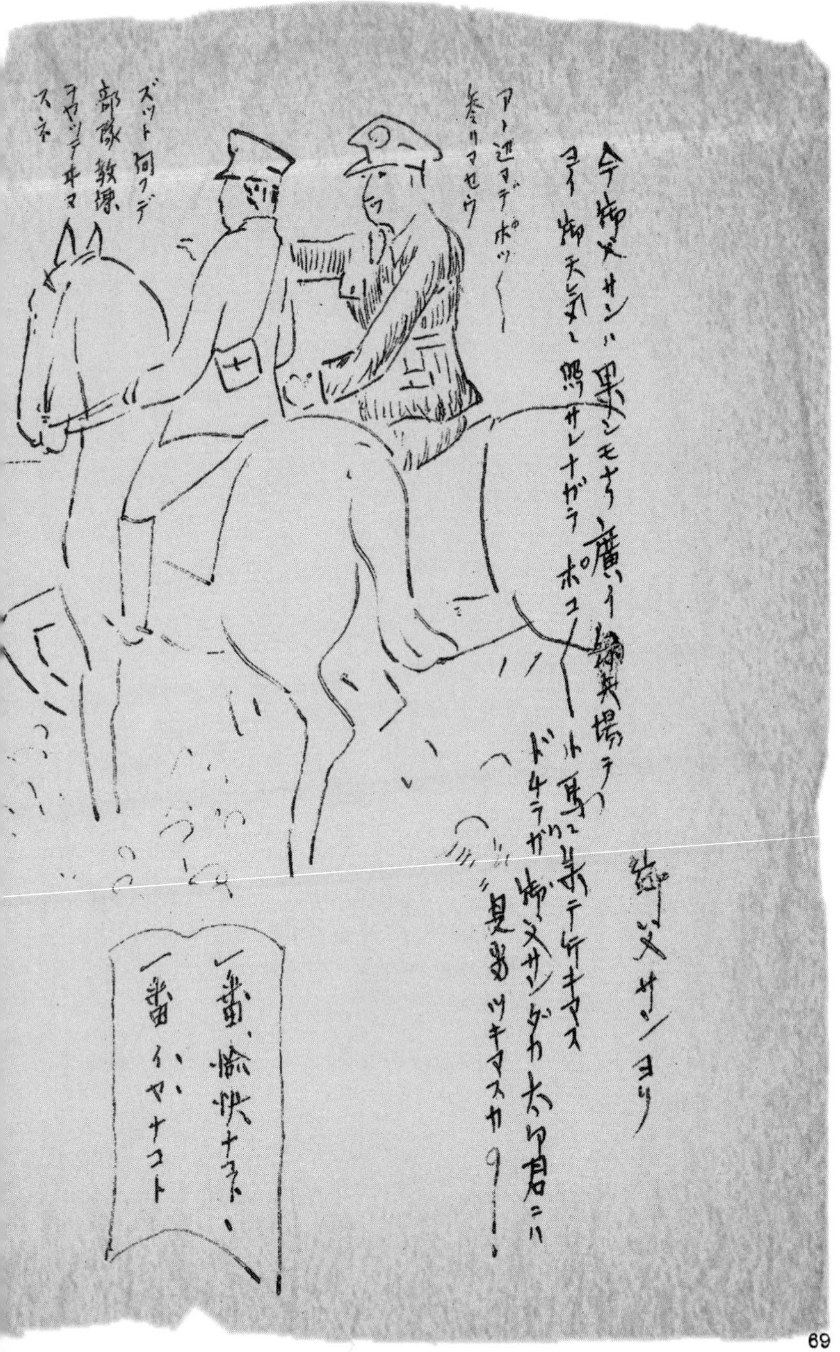

今御父サンハ果シテ乗リモセウ廣イ練兵場ヲ

ヨイ御天気ニ鳴サレナガラポヨ〰ト馬ニ乗テ行キマス

ドチラガ御父サンダカ分ツ君ニハ

アー迷ヒマデポツ〰

参リマセウ

是非ツキマスカ〰

御父サンノヨリ

ズツト何クデ部隊教練ヲヤツテ居マスネ

一番、愉快ナコト、

一番イヤナコト

— To Taro —

MY FAVORITE PASTIME vs. MY WORST NIGHTMARE:
From Father

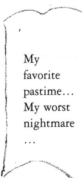

My
favorite
pastime...
My worst
nightmare
...

I am on my horse, loping across a big parade
ground filled with sunshine.
Can you point out your father?
I will make my way to the other side of the
field.
A military drill is being held in the distance.

Here, let me
teach you...

No, I'm afraid I
really cannot...

Oh, don't be shy...

Every Friday, there is a dance for
the officers and their families. I
am mortified.
Can you tell which one your
father is?

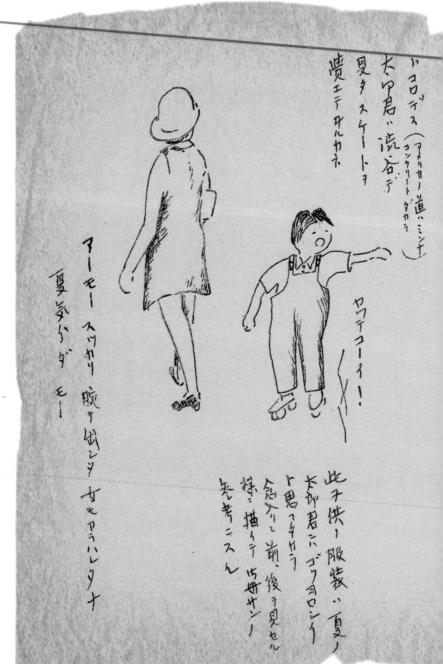

コチラハ
大変暖カダカラ
子供達ハ皆
外ニ出テ大騒ギヲ
シテ遊ンデ居マス
キレイ道ノ真中ニデ
スケートヲヤウテ井ル

ソラ行クゾ
ソラ〳〵

二月十六日

御父サンヨリ

73

Summer has suddenly arrived and children scamper outside to play.

These are children roller skating in the middle of the street
(American streets are all paved in concrete).
Taro, do you remember the skaters we saw in Shibuya?

I think this child's outfit would be comfortable for Taro to wear in
the summer. I'm drawing it in detail, front and back, for your
mother's benefit.

Ah, summer is upon us—I see a
woman in a sleeveless dress.

坊が居ルバイクシテ
余モデャルダ、ガ ×
ドーゾ 9・・・
・・ありメーリカ ネ

最新型、四人乗リ
色モ形モ比通リ
デス（此塩ハ見かけ図から
切り取リ貼り候と見せ
様ト思フテ）

太郎君へ

御父サンハ今度コンナイ、自動車ヲ買ッタ

外出シタシビニ坊ヲ買ッテヤッタ　ト違ッタゾマ　連モ高ッダマ

御父サンハ今自動車ヲ有ッテ運轉シテ氏ハ

御父サンヨリ

77

HOW ABOUT A RIDE: To Taro, from Father

I went and bought myself a fine car.

It's not like the toy cars I bought for you on our outings, Taro.
It's quite expensive.

I drive on my own now.

If you were here, I'd let you ride along as much as you wanted.
How about a ride?

It's the newest model and can seat four. The color and shape
are just like in this picture. (I clipped the picture out of a
brochure to show you.)

America in the latter half of the 1920s

On October 24, 1929, Kuribayashi was at Ft. Riley, Kansas. It was then that the New York Stock Market started to crash. Kuribayashi's letters, however, hardly touched on the repercussions felt across the entire nation. There is just one illustration that depicts two barefooted brothers cowering in the dark that is suggestive of the grave state of affairs. Of course, Kuribayashi's letters were written to a preschooler for the purpose of assuring him about his father's well-being. Perhaps Kuribayashi didn't want to discuss anything that would worry the child. On the other hand, he gave detailed descriptions of his acquaintances and the people he saw on the street.

Until the Great Depression hit in 1929, America was enjoying a peaceful period, her "Indian Summer," as it were. Automobiles and radio were popular, and everyone was still celebrating Charles Lindbergh's historic trans-Atlantic flight. The next year, the first Academy Awards ceremony was held, followed by the debut of Mickey Mouse.

Women had already won the right to vote, and short hair and shorter skirts became mainstream. Kuribayashi's drawing of the woman in a sleeveless dress (page 73) is an example of the new trend in women's wear.

The Depression brought an abrupt halt to the American economy. Small-scale farmers felt the pinch as well as bigger industries involved with textiles, coalmining and railroading. Things were bad until President Franklin Roosevelt introduced his New Deal Policy in 1933.

AMERICAN GIRLS ARE DIFFERENT: March 3, to Taro, from Father in Ft. Bliss, Texas

81

AMERICAN GIRLS ARE DIFFERENT: March 3, to Taro,
from Father in Ft. Bliss, Texas

"Mother, is it all right if I show Capt. Kuribayashi how I dance. La-di-la-di-laa…"

"American girls are different from birth," your father thinks to himself.

Captain Weitman's daughter is nine years old.
When the music starts to play, she starts to twirl.

Now, this is quite a [traffic] jam we have here.

Getting into an accident and having my name in the papers would be embarrassing. I'll take it easy, very easy.

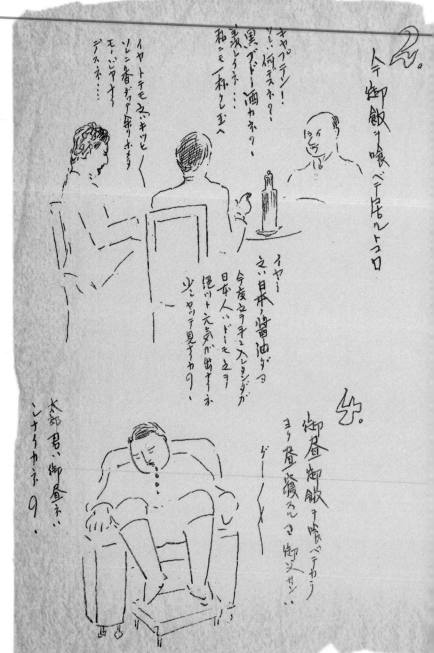

今御飯ヲ喰ベテ居ルトコロ

2a.

キャプテン！
コレハ何デスネ？
黒ブドー酒カネ？、
裏トウネ・・・
私モ一杯クレへ

イヤ、コレハ、何デスネ？・

イヤ　トテモ、エヽキツト
ソレハ香ガァテ余リ、ウマク
モ、ハジヤナイ
デスネ・・・

イヤー
えヽ日本ノ醤油ダマ
今度カラモット　スメヲシンダガ
日本人ハ　ドーモ、コレヲ
塗ツテ元気ガ出ますネ
少シ　ヤッテ見ますカ、、

4.

御昼御飯ヲ喰ベテカラ
キョウ　昼寝ヲシテ　御ジサン、、

ゲー、ゲー

御昼御飯ヲ喰ベテカラ
キョウ　昼寝ヲスルマ　御ジサン、、

太郎　君ハ　御昼ネハ
シナイカネ？9

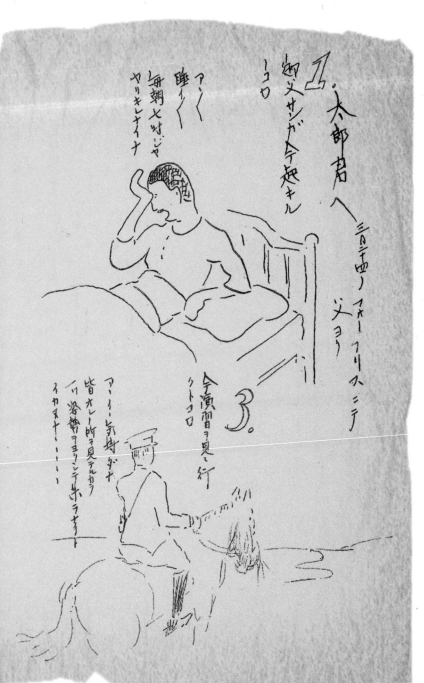

DRIVING: March 24, to Taro, from Father in Ft. Bliss, Texas

This is your father as he tries to get up.

Ahh, I am sleepy. Rising at seven every morning is an ordeal.

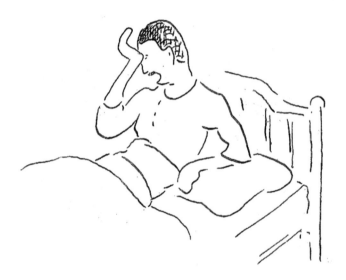

Here is your
father as he
eats his meal.

"Oh, this is
strong stuff.
And I don't care
for the
fragrance..."

"Captain! What is
this? Black wine? I say,
it looks good...don't
mind if I try some."

"No, sir. This is
Japanese soy sauce. It
gives a Japanese man
energy. Would you like
to give it a try?"

This is your father on his way to inspect a
military drill.

Ah, this is nice.
I feel everybody's eyes on me...I'd better sit up
straight in the saddle.

Your father often steals a few winks after lunch. Zzzzzzz...

Taro, do you often nap?

デモ コンテニ 上手ニナント

猶リジャツマラナイナ

太郎君ガ居タ分

柳本サンノ右ヘ坐ラセルンダガ

ソンデ左ギキト柳本サン、バ

後、坐席ガ……

ドウ今度ハ……ソノ面

ニマハウテ行ッテ見様リ

イ、マシンバイダ

ヤア逆モ別嬢夫ガ行ッテ

ソンデ乱暴ナ際ンカ、ドウダイ

今度、アンコウ曲ローカ

ヤツ、メチコ人チ供ゲ

先ク〜〜 ブー〜〜

ヤマシン 云ッテヤラ

ナント ケテス

根ガ俺ノ様ニ丈夫

ヤ、デナイカラナ

太郎事ヲ

注意セヌト

隠レ乍モ

赤ボニ話ツテ

コンデマシタ……

ソレカラ 自魚ツテブ

書ニ送ッテヤラロト云ッテ

ナイカ

黙ッテサルト、ホント 何ヲ送ッテ

今サ云ワライ、ソレニ此頃ハ手供モ

ニ一モ一會モ、デタンカ十八日ガ、中々ヨコシヤ

キレドモ十九日モダイ……

ケテス

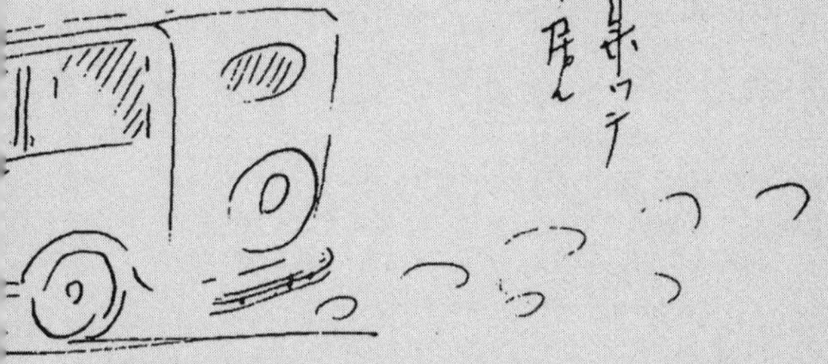

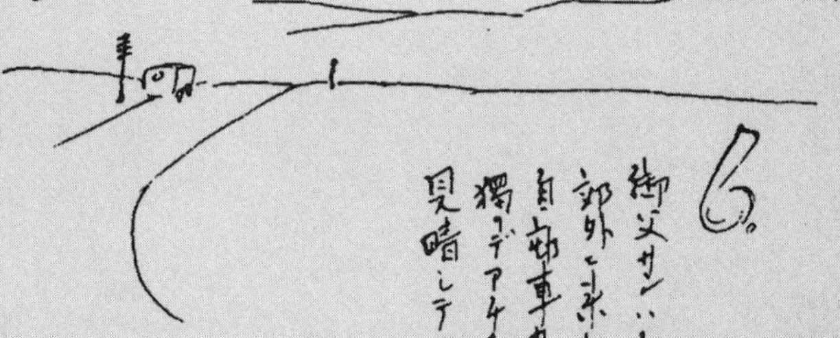

I am going for a spin today.

Perhaps I'll try to pick up some speed.
It's very pleasant—it's like you almost slide along.
I have become such an expert driver. I only wish I were not alone.
If you were here, Taro, I would put you in the passenger's seat.
Yoko and your mother would be in the back...
Let's see now, which direction should I turn?

It's a good day for taking a spin—not too many people out.
Ah, now there are some very pretty girls.
And there's a reckless driver.
I think I'll make a turn here.
Oops! I just missed hitting a Mexican child. Careful! Honk, honk.

Your father is in the suburbs and getting out of the car to take in the view.

It's a grand view, but a little hazy.
That hill must be in Mexican territory. A civil war is going on there.

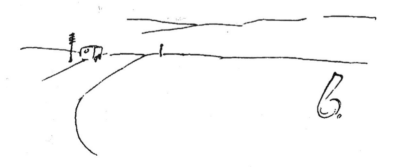

I am at my desk writing a letter.

It is late at night.

I cannot say enough about keeping fit because not everyone is as robust as I.

Also, please watch over Taro carefully.

All right now, enough about the baby...

May I also ask that you send me some fish and seaweed once in a while.

Must I ask before I receive anything?

And letters are infrequent these days.

I have not received a letter in eighteen days now. It will be the nineteenth day come tomorrow.

Horses and a Chevrolet

Kuribayashi was an excellent equestrian. He had written that his "worst nightmare" was dancing, and his favorite pastime was riding (page 68). He was said to have tamed a wild horse named Tento while he was attending the Cavalry Academy.

Kuribayashi purchased a Chevrolet in 1929. The Chevrolet K was introduced four years earlier in a bid to outsell Ford's Model T, which claimed fifty-six percent of the market. In a short time, Chevrolet sales gained momentum and two years later, production of the Model T came to a halt. Ford no longer was the biggest manufacturer of automobiles. As luck would have it, Kuribayashi was driving a car that was the symbol of a turning point in the American automobile industry.

At that time, modernization was at the top of the Japanese army's list of priorities. Against such a backdrop, the cavalry was contemplating replacing its stable of horses with a fleet of automobiles. What was going through Kuribayashi's mind as he took his frequent drives and made the motor trip from Ft. Riley, Kansas, to Washington, D.C. (page 184)? At Iwo Jima, Kuribayashi told one of his men that the "American military has an amazing relationship with big industries. In an automated auto factory in Detroit, the entire operation could be started with a single push of a button. An industrialist becomes Secretary of the Army and Navy and as a result, munitions factories are backing the military. How can you beat something like that?"

Kuribayashi was keenly aware of the mechanization of weapon production in the U.S., and, at the same time, the structural problems faced by the Japanese army. On the other hand, he was in the habit of asking valets to "Please tie my car," rather than ask that it be parked. He would probably have been hard-pressed to make a choice between horses and cars.

レデイ！
待テ、ドモ〜
皆ヲキョウソウ
（英語デ）

諸君〜
午後ノ賞品ハ
素敵ナシナジナ
（スペイン語デ）

子供
ワー〜ガー〜
ベタ〜〜
『スペイン語ト英語ト！
方言許リ使ウカラ
御父サンニハ中々ワカラヌ〜』

太郎君へ

ヽ　コレハ御父サンガ
五十哩モアル知長節
、式場ヘ行ックトコロ

五十哩ト遠インデスネ
但シ比河子ダト
一時半モ
ヘリマセンカネ
途中景色モ
イ・カラ　ユックリ
連レテ行クデスヨ

大人三人　子供三人
ヲ余セルト車ガ
ズット重クナルワ～

フォート・ブリス　ニテ　五月二十―

父ヨリ

御父サンガ、俳鬼大忙デ
運動会ヲヤッテ井ル
トコロ

太郎君ハ運動ヲ好キナラナイト
イケナイゾ
ドンガオ父サンデセウノ、

今度ハ　旗取リカクレ
軍人サンガ言戦気ッテ見ルベ
野所夫　天気ガ
イ・ヤ

久シ振ッテ日本ノ
軍人サンヲ見テ
セイクシタ

何時軍服ヲ御カス
ニナリタバデ
ヤウネ

日本ノ旗

アメリカノ旗

メキシユノ旗

GOING TO AN ATHLETIC MEET: May 2, to Taro,
from Father in Ft. Bliss, Texas

This is your father on his way to a celebration
marking the emperor's birthday, to be held in a place
fifty miles away.

Fifty miles is a good distance but we should make it
in an hour and a half.
The scenery is nice so please take your time.

We have three grownups and three children in our
group, making the car quite heavy.
Honk! Honk!

Is the next competition "grab-the-flag"?
They are all excited that a real soldier is leading
them.
When did he change into his uniform, I wonder?

Mexican
flag

American
flag

Japanese
flag

Your father is shouting orders to the kids at the athletic meet.
You must develop a liking for sports, too, Taro.

Can you tell which one your father is?

It's been a while since I had the pleasure of seeing a Japanese soldier.

Miss! Wait, wait, wait!
You start at the whistle. (in English)
Everybody! We have great prizes for you. (in Spanish)

Children: Blah, blah, blah...
(They are speaking in a dialect mixing Spanish and English. I do not
understand a single word.)

THE DOGS HERE UNDERSTAND ONLY ENGLISH:
May 23, to Taro, from Father in Ft. Bliss, Texas

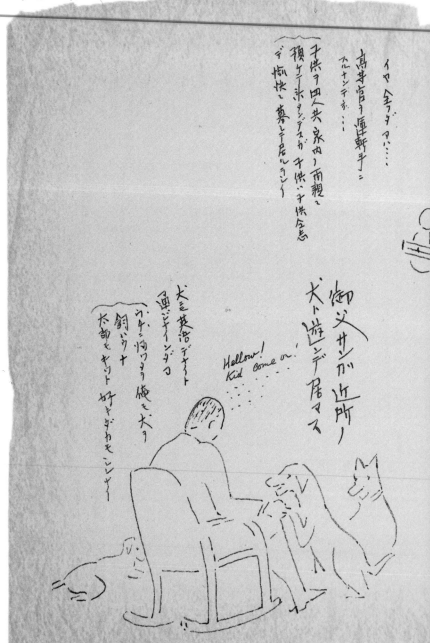

イヤ　全ク　ダ　ハ・・・・

高等官ヲ　運転手ニ

プルナンテネ・・・

子供ヲ四人共　泉カニ雨親ニ

積ケテ来　タンデスガ　子供ハ子供今志

（デ愉快ニ　夢ヒテ居ルラシイ）

犬ニ英語デナート

御ニデナイト　ダメ

ウチニ帰ッタラ　俺モ犬ヲ

飼イタイナ

犬ヲ御モ　キット　好キダヰモ　シレナイ

御父サンガ　近所ノ

犬ト遊ンデ　居マス

Hellow!
Kid come on.

太郎君へ

五月二十シテ

フオートブリス ニテ 父より

御父サンが今デ、"メキシコ"カラ"モハバソ"ニ

旅行ニ来タ メキシコ公使館ハ御父ー

竹下海軍中佐夫妻ヲ見物ニ連レテマハッテ居マス。

御父サン曰ク

コトニテ 一日中御案内

レテ タクト 三、四十ドルノ

駄賃ヲ 貰ッテコロ、デスネ

アハ・・・

栗栖サンガメキシコニ御住デ

ナウナ゛デ 主ニ 運転手ヲ

セサスカラ 其時マデ

此ヤ脈賃、拝借シ

テ置キマスワ

オホ・・・

私ハ妻子ニ 週ラ十日毎ニ

手紙ヲ出シマス

子供ノ字ガヨメルカラ下手ナ

（画ヲカイテ ヤリマスツ）

兄ハ私ガ達筆ニナト

子供ニ手紙ヤラナイ

（デ困ルンデスヨ）

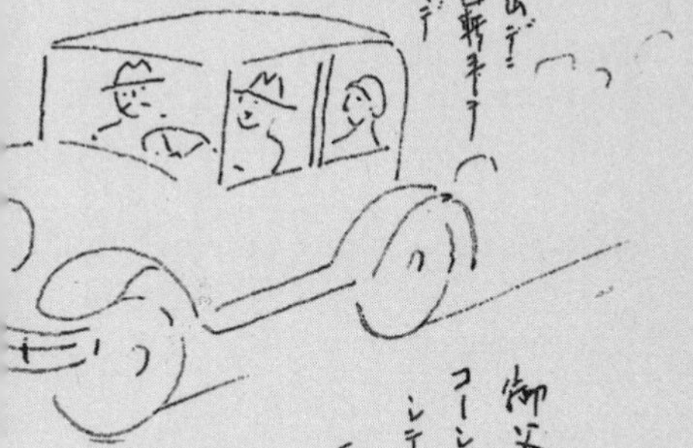

101

THE DOGS HERE UNDERSTAND ONLY ENGLISH:
May 23, to Taro, from Father in Ft. Bliss, Texas

Your father is now taking Lieutenant Colonel Takeshita [navy] and his wife on a sightseeing tour. Takeshita is a military attaché at the Japanese Embassy in Mexico. He and his wife are visiting El Paso, Texas.

"Mr. Kuribayashi, next time you come to Mexico, I'll have my husband drive you around. Until then, we owe you (laughing)."

"My husband never writes to the children unless I prod him."

"You're right (chuckling). You have a high-ranking officer as your chauffeur."

"We left our four children with my wife's folks. The children seem to be enjoying themselves."

Your father says: "I hope you realize that this tour is going to cost you thirty to forty dollars (laughing)."

"I make it a point to write home every week or every ten days. My son doesn't read yet, so I make clumsy drawings."

THE DOGS HERE UNDERSTAND ONLY ENGLISH:
May 23, to Taro, from Father in Ft. Bliss, Texas

Your father is playing with the neighbor's dog.

Dogs only understand English here.

Perhaps I'll get a dog when I return home.
Taro would probably like that.

Hello!
Kid come on!

Ft. Bliss and Ft. Riley

Kuribayashi was at Ft. Bliss from the end of 1928 and Ft. Riley from August 1929.

The word "fort" implies a military base and it is followed by the name of the area. In his letters, Kuribayashi's rendering in katakana of "Riley" sometimes differs.

Ft. Bliss is in the state of Texas, northeast of El Paso, located near the Mexican border. Ft. Riley is located west of Kansas City, the capital of the state of Kansas. Kuribayashi gives the distance from Kansas City as one hundred and fifty miles. What is described as a "very small country town" (page 148) must be the town of Riley, north of Ft. Riley.

It is believed that Kuribayashi had quarters at the fort and he would sometimes make trips into town. He also talks about dining at the home of Dr. Furukochi and his wife (page 128). Furukochi was a doctor who ministered not only to the Japanese-American community but to poor Mexican-Americans as well. During his incarceration at the outbreak of World War II, he continued to provide medical care for his fellow countrymen. Back in El Paso after the war, he directed his attention to the poor and needy. In 1960, he was decorated by the Japanese government in recognition for his services. The Furukochis were also thought to have provided Kuribayashi with much-needed Japanese conversation and food.

RAW FISH AND PICKLED CUCUMBERS:
July 20, to Taro, from Father in El Paso

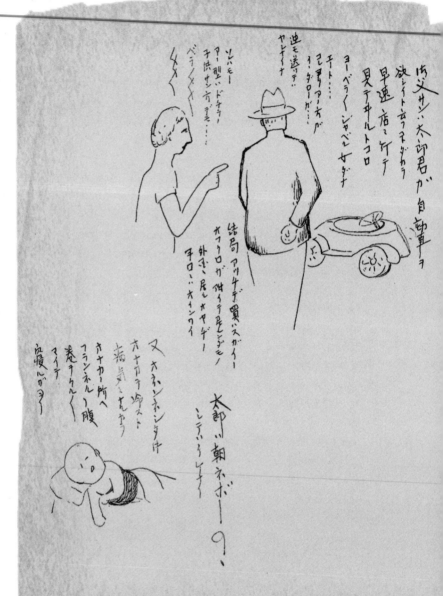

太郎君へ

七月二十一
えんピツテ　父より

オ父サンハ一軒ノアパートメントニ住ッテ

身軽デ誰ニデモ見エナイカラ

素ッパダカニナレマス

立チナガラ日本ヲ切ット食ジゲナイ

楽シコンナ格好ニモント一層

大サジミ・キウリモミ、ビール新夏...

シカラシレハト思ッテステホテタラヲナ

ア・唾ヲ...込ム　ゴクリ...

RAW FISH AND PICKLED CUCUMBERS:

July 20, to Taro, from Father in El Paso

Your father lives in an apartment and since there is nobody around, I can strip to my underwear.

Now that's better...I feel as if I am in Japan.
But sitting like this reminds me of the food I am missing...
Sashimi [raw fish], kyurimomi [pickled cucumbers], beer, clams...

I find it hard to bear...ah, I am drooling.

I am at a store, looking for the toy car you seem to want.

The saleswoman is quite a talker.
Uh…
"I wonder if this one would be better."
"I don't know if it can be sent overseas."

"That model is one that any youngster would love to have…
yakkity yak yak yak…so on and so forth."

Now that I think of it, it may be better to buy it in Japan.
You're going to have to ask your mother…your father can't
handle this from abroad.

RAW FISH AND PICKLED CUCUMBERS:
July 20, to Taro, from Father in El Paso

Try not to sleep in, Taro.

Keep your tummy warm while you sleep so you won't get sick.
Wrap a flannel cloth around your stomach when you go to bed.

A German shepherd named Marie

Kuribayashi often mentioned animals such as squirrels, cats, and dogs in his letters. "Cats seem like the only friends I have," he said in a wistful moment (page 21). Later, he played with a neighbor's dog and murmured, "Perhaps I'll get myself a dog when I return home." (page 101). According to his daughter, Takako, Kuribayashi spent many years with an intelligent military dog that he named Marie. However, it is uncertain if the German shepherd sitting next to Kuribayashi in the center of this photograph is Marie.

In the letters he sent to Takako from Iwo Jima, Kuribayashi often wrote of a hen and her family. He continued to have a soft spot for God's gentler creatures, even in the midst of a vicious war.

Early June, 1943, in Canton (now Guangzhou)

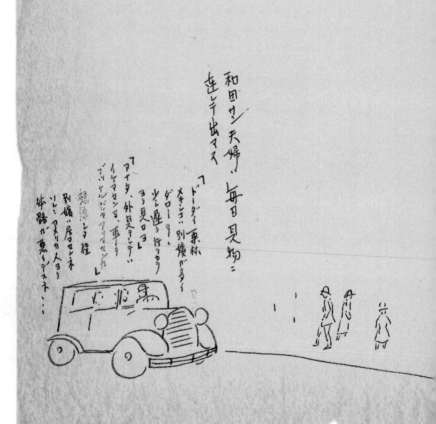

和田サン夫婦ハ毎日見物ニ
連レテ出マス

「ドーダイ栗林
メキシコニ別嬢ガタイ
ゲローり、
少シ違ウ行ッタラ
ヨリ見ロヨ

「アイタ、外見テレテハ
イケマセンヨ、車ヲ
ブツケルバカリデス...

「想像ス程
別嬢ガ居マセネ
ソレ、アメリカ人ヨリ
体路ガ悪ウデスネ...

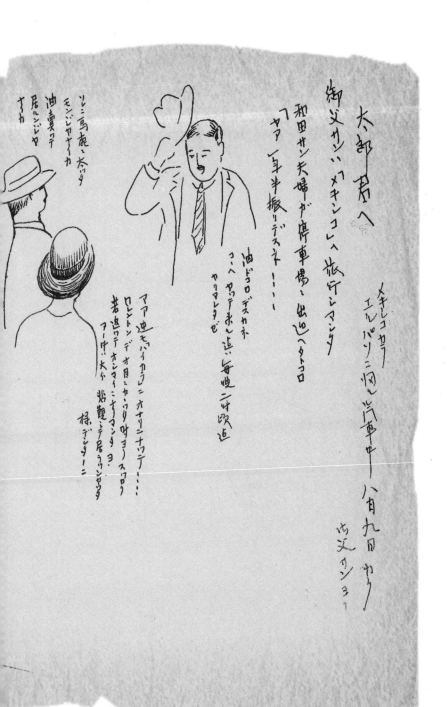

Your father took a trip to Mexico.
Here are Mr. and Mrs. Wada meeting me at the train station.

"Oh, how smart you look...
You look so much younger than when we met in Washington.
You sounded rather pessimistic at the time."

"You've put on weight.
You must be loafing around."

"I haven't seen you in a year and a half...Loafing around? Yes, until
two in the morning before I got here."

The Wadas take me out sightseeing every day.

"Well, so what do you think, Kuribayashi?
Mexico has a lot of beautiful women, eh?"

"I'll drive slowly so you can take a good look.
Dear, keep your eyes on the road, please. You'll run into
something."

There are not as many pretty women as I imagined.
And they are not as well built as Americans...

アナタコトヲ抱持待會ニスル件ハ
和田サンノ家デクツロイダ
気、ナレマス

此頃ハ、ジャ刺身ヲ上手
ニ作シ
調子ガ・・・

メキシコ料理ダト
女中ガ二人モ居ンデスカラ
スツカリヤカロラレマスワ
せし、実ハ昼食ヲぬきマスデ
私モ中々働ケミ己マス

ミモ上手復カヘリアレモ上
復ケアート另ヒマストゝ
時日ガ足リナイデ私用
トマリマスリ

ヘ出テ次第デオ父サンハ途中
一音号今中泊つとセンテナイマス

コーヒーテモ
中ゝ上手ニ出来ミズ
此塩昆布ガ行ヨーデス
ハアヱ鞠一味覚漬デスカ

ビールモオセハイ日本ヨリ
以来ハシメメテ ナンデスヨ

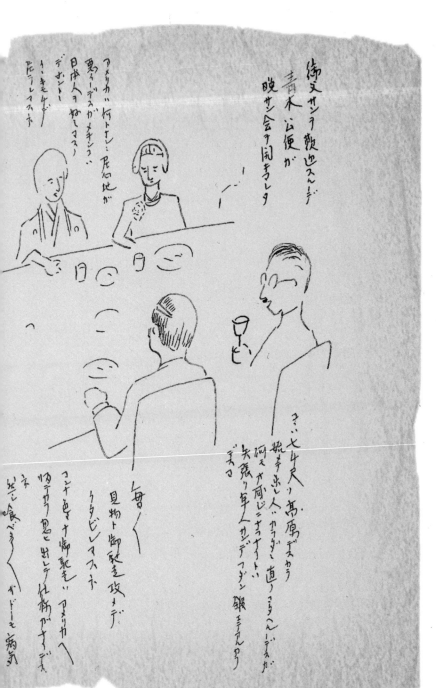

御文サンヲ敷ヰスンデ
青木公使ガ
晩サン会ヲ開キマシタ

アメリカハ何トヰニ尼クレガ
黒イラデスガメチャンコヰ
日本人ヲ招モマス/
デ、ヰント、
ニチキナガ
左ニコレイマスネ

ミ、七尺ノ高原デスカラ
脱キ出シ人ハカラダニ直ノ、シランデスガ
何レガ局ジニナラナイト、
矢張リ年ムサンデハダン鏡ヰヰんヤ
デス/

毎ク
見物ト御延速攻メデ
クタビレマスネ
コレ専ヤ御駄走リアメリカヘ
帰テカラ君ト出シテ仕納ガすぐデ
ス、
ミシ喰ベテ、ザドーモ病気

Consul Aoki had a dinner party to welcome your father.

Living in America can be uncomfortable but Mexicans are fond of the Japanese, so I find it quite nice here.

This city is located seven thousand feet above sea level, and first-time visitors are often affected by it.

"You say you do not feel anything. It must be all the training you have had as a military man."

I am tired from all the daily sightseeing and the plates of good food.

The memories of all this good food will haunt me after I return to America. This obsession with food will be my downfall...

When there are no social commitments, I relax at the Wada household.

"We have two maids and so I leave the Mexican cooking to them. But my husband prefers Japanese meals and keeps me busy. I'd like you to try this and that and everything else, but I'm afraid you haven't enough time."

Before he knew it, your father had stayed for two nights.

She can even slice sashimi [raw fish] well these days.

This is very good coffee. I like this salted seaweed very much.
Oh, is this snapper marinated in miso?
I have not had beer and raw fish since I left Japan.

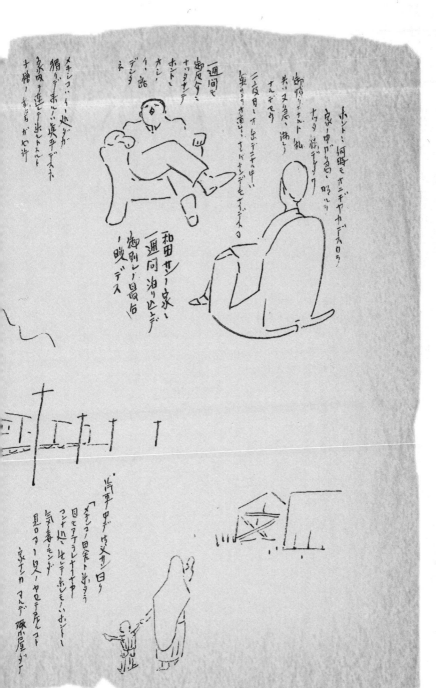

ホント、何時モオニギヤカデスカラ
家ノ中ガニギヤカ、明ルク

御病気ニナルト私
共ハ又々忙シ、淋シ
ナンテオモイヲリ

二夜目ハオトナシャ中
楽々ナ夜ヲ、サバナンデモナラデスの

一週間デ
御見ウ二
ナッタサミ
ホント
オレ、
イ、話
デショ
ネ

和田サン一家ハ
一週間泊リコンデ
御別レノ最后ノ
一晩デス

汽車ノ中デ付父サン曰ク
「メキシコ一周先ト出タラウ
目デアテラレナイナヤ
コレ位、セレテホレモナイホント、
気ヲ毒モノデ
見ロコレ父、ヤセテ居ルコト、
家ナシカマンデ職内屋ダデ

メキシコ、イ、処ダガ
猾リテ来ない真平デスた
家内ヲ連レテ来ルトスルト
十軒ノ処ラガ50許

121

It is the last night of my one-week stay with the Wadas.

Your presence brightened up our home.
We will certainly miss you.
On your second visit, please feel free to bring your wife.

How would you feel about being assigned to the Japanese Legation?
If you're not fussy about where you live, living abroad is as good an option as any.

Forgive me for taking advantage of your hospitality and staying for a whole week.

Mexico is a nice place, but living here alone does not appeal to me.
But if I bring the wife, I'd be worried about my children's education…
No, I don't think a post overseas would be a good idea.

Your father muses on the train...
"The Mexican countryside is pathetic. I feel sorry for those who are born here. Look how skinny that poor child is. The houses look like pigsties. Taro is fortunate not to have been born here."

The train is taking your father to America.

There is a company of soldiers on every train. That's because there are bandits.

ニーム
一度、チニ百哩ハ哩
アルナ
えい中々大仕事ダゾ
ソレニ
人家ナキ沙漠ヲ大都
横断セネバナランカラナ
廾自イマア「ペコス」泊リカナ……ドレソレデ
其町ノ様子ヲ一寸調べテ見様ゎ……
………………………

太郎君へ
ハカニテイシン

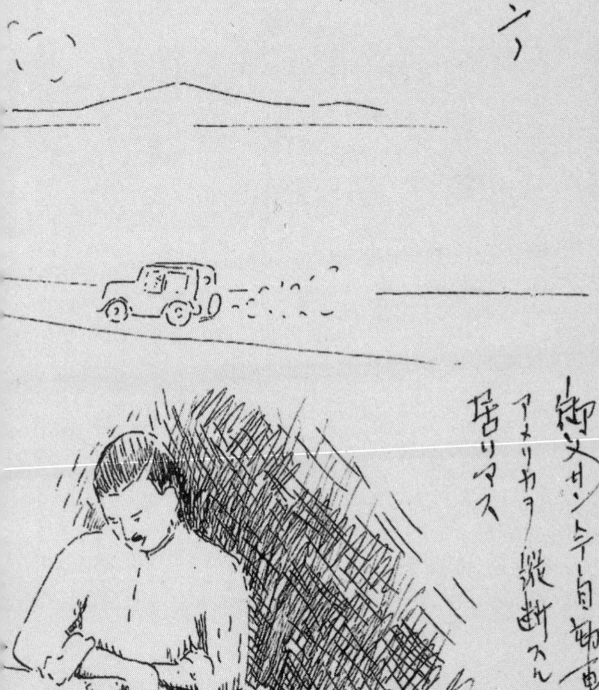

御父サン今日自動車デ
アメリカヲ縦断スル計画ヲシテ
居リマス

Today your father is making plans to travel across
America by car.

Hmmmm. There are exactly 1,246 miles. This is going
to be a big undertaking. And there are a lot of
uninhabited deserts along the way.
I'll spend the first night in Pecos...
I'll have to check up on the area...

"The Marching Song for Horses"

Kuribayashi took up the shakuhachi (five-holed vertical bamboo) while he was in middle school and continued to play it often. He carried it with him to America, but "the maid mistakenly burned it in the fireplace," his daughter Takako explains. The woman is depicted in the illustrated letter on page 140. Kuribayashi was also an accomplished chanter of Chinese poems. He often sang Takako to sleep with "Moon on a Rainy Night." A horse that Kuribayashi was fond of is mentioned in this song.

In 1939, Kuribayashi was the section chief for equine matters at the Ministry of the Army. As part of a project for "Horse's Day," he invited the public to send in songs to commemorate the event. He is said to have added a phrase to the selected song: "blood runs through the reins from my arms." "The Marching Song for Horses" was announced and a recording was made by Taro Shoji. One wonders what kind of music Kuribayashi listened to during his stay overseas.

Committee to select the Marching Song for "Horse's Day." Starting from the fifth person from the left, front row: composer Yuji Koseki, composer Kosaku Yamada, composer Shinpei Nakayama, Kuribayashi.

THEY ARE VERY CAUTIOUS—I AM IMPRESSED:
To Taro, from Father in Ft. Bliss, Texas

何？滋ハ綾カラ
帰リダヨ。
ジャ オマヘ近
連レテカヘテ上ゲヤ
御ウチヘ、ドツチヘノ

比ゞサン腹ノ中デ
「ナーンダ馬ノ子ハ
自動車ナンゾ珍ラカナインゾ
イーヤ ヨソノ人マデ
貰ツテカドワカサレ タヤ
イケネェト思ツテヰルンダ
中々用心深ウ
感心〱〱〱」

失敬〱

太郎君ヘ
此ノ供ノ様ニ
御母サンノ云フコトヲ
ヨクキクコト
御父サンノ様ニ
御飯ヲドツサリ
喰ベルコト
ソーシテ キツト
大キクナツテ サウラテ ハイケサウ

難有ウ御ヂサンハ
ケレド僕達ハ
泳グ代リニ
ヨソノ御ヂサンニハ
乗セテ頂イテ
イケナイコト
比母サンガ云フカラ

ウチノ家ニハ居ルカ
「ヂサンガダイナヨ」ツテ
マスマ
オ父ト文ハ日本ヘノ
一番ヂィ・デスネ……
日本ノ御居デ居ラット ボンド
毎晩 テモ タベテ チカヒシャレ
ルテ 外ヨリ 御ットメンジャ！
香ク「ヂャガラ」モ攻メデ
ネー……ハーーシ二モ
モー 馴レ アレヌカ？

此ノ意味ハ今
太ロ君ニハカラナイ
カラ尚々ニシルベ

此ノ意味ハ今
太ロ君ニハカラナイ
カラ尚々ニシルベ

太郎君へ

フォートブラグ

父ヨリ

何時モ御飛走コチコエラ古河双トオフ

御殿西巻サン夫婦ー御カ4ーデ

何時夕ベテ オザシミ セモウマリツデス

熱日本ミ兄ト 毎晩ヤシリーーリデスナ

コノ胡爪デスナ コレモ逃キナンデスヨ

ハー若芽ー御ウエミデスネ

コビカラヲタ ラーンジソーデスコ

熱 何食サヤラナヤデニ三度ヘ

食事中ヤ ヤラヤシデスコ

一二四多0上デ

御父サンハ ヨソノ

御ウチデ中キ

オ、バス、シテ

チマス、キテ

豊津メンデス

半斗内州

立ハ御父サンガ ドライブヨシテ

アメリカー子供弄ト遊シテオル

トコロ

ネー

姉ッチャンカ、ホントー

御父サンヲ待コアヤラッシャルデショウ

私ー子供ガナイガ

モーヘ 何スー

悲レイン

デスノ

殊ニ外ヲ

二足ント

サア末王へ

オチチサンガ

日申車ー

乗セテヤンカウ

THEY ARE VERY CAUTIOUS—I AM IMPRESSED:
To Taro, from Father in Ft. Bliss, Texas

This is your father talking to some American children during his drive.

Come, I'll give you a ride.
What? You're on your way home?
Then I'll give you a lift.
Which direction are you heading?

Thank you, sir. But we'll walk home.
Mother says not to accept rides from strangers.
Sorry, sorry, sorry.

Your father thinks to himself,
"I see, cars are nothing new to American children.
No, no, that's not it. They think they'll be kidnapped hopping
into a stranger's car. They are very cautious. I am impressed."

Taro, you too must mind your mother.
Eat well like your father.
And the next time I see you, you will no doubt have grown into
a big boy.

THEY ARE VERY CAUTIOUS—I AM IMPRESSED:
To Taro, from Father in Ft. Bliss, Texas

Here I am at the home of Dr. and Mrs. Furukochi where I am
often invited to dine.

"Your son and the rest of your family must miss you.
You've no idea how much I regret not having had children.
Especially here in a foreign country."

My wife makes sashimi [sliced raw fish] very well.
It suits the Japanese palate...
You'd have this every night in Japan.
Here you must face heaps of potatoes, day in and day out...
Ha ha! Have you gotten used to it?

Sashimi tastes good anytime.
In Japan, I have it every night.
This is cucumber. It is one of my favorites.
Oh! Seaweed soup. They say it is good for your health.

I don't eat between meals, but I eat a fair amount at each meal.
I tell people this in advance. I eat a large amount at other
people's tables.
(Is this one of your father's strategies?)
(Since Taro will not understand the meaning of this, I will cross
it out.)

TREATS FOR THE NEWSPAPER BOY

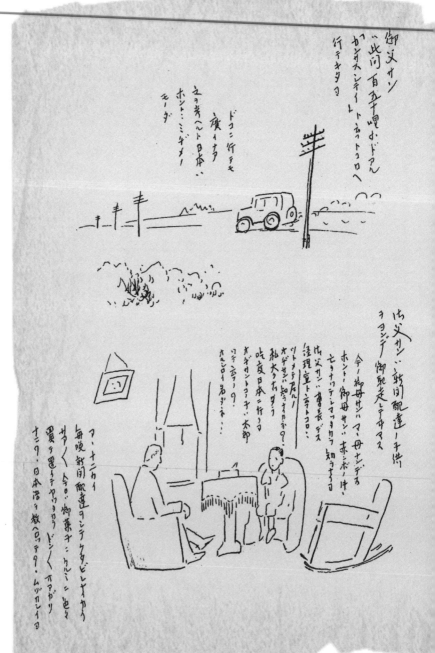

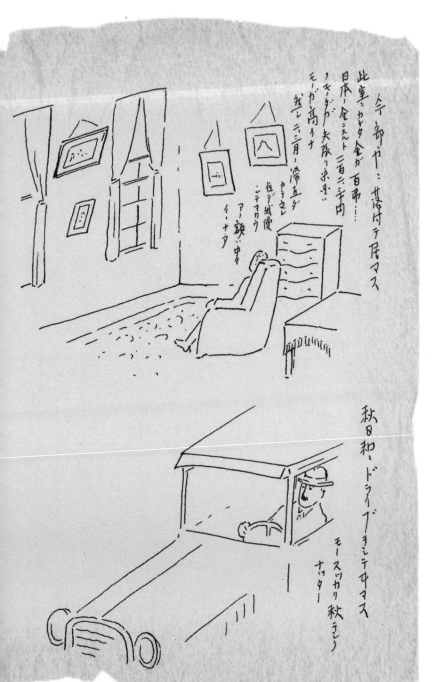

TREATS FOR THE NEWSPAPER BOY

I am relaxing in my room now.

I have spent $100 on this room.
Converted into yen, it comes to ¥220 or ¥230.
Yes, America is expensive.
I'll only be here for two or three months, so this will
have to do.
That frame looks good hanging over there.

Taking a drive in fine autumn weather.

It's autumn everywhere you look.

TREATS FOR THE NEWSPAPER BOY

The other day, your father went to Kansas City, a city about one hundred and fifty miles away.

There are wide open spaces everywhere you look.
Compared to this, Japan is pitiful.

Your father invited the newspaper boy over for a
treat.

I live with my stepmother.
My real mother died when I was a baby so I don't
know her at all.
My father is a sergeant. He works in a place called
the accounting department.

Have you heard of it?
When I grow up, I'd like to go to Japan.
Your son's name is Taro? What a funny name...

Don't you get tired of delivering newspapers every evening?
Come now, I bought cakes, walnuts and lots of other goodies just
for you.
Help yourself.
What's that? You want to learn Japanese. That would be
difficult, I'm afraid.

エ、子供モ アルッテ？・・マア二人モ・・・・

私ノ夫ハ 陸軍伍長ダヨ 中タイ・〇〇男ダヨ
子供ハ ドーモ ナイネ・・・・・

目方ヲ・・・三十二貫ア
ルンデスヨ
コレヲ・此文身ハ若イ

男ラヤッター・ダマ
女中カネ？ノ・軍人サンノ家行ク

渡リアルイテ イ度 三十年 勤メタコトニナルネ

日本ハイ、近カネ？・・・・・・・
・・・〇〇・・

私ダンス、進ニ素朴ノ ナンデスヨ
若ノ付ニ会ウマガウタンデスヨ・・
（特ニカヨスニラ言ヒマシタ）

御父サンガ今夜来タ
女中ノ角力様ナ
御父サント話ランテヰマス
此オ嬢サン・夫ハ御父サンガ今居ル 珠縁ノ
不土宵デス

御父サン腹ノ中デ
マルデ和ン牛海ダネ
コレデモ 断髮七三分ケカ・・
ソレ又ヨクシャベル婆ダナ
英語ハゲニゴニヤッタリ ウボハシ
ニナッタ イ度スハイ・ワオ⊠

［太郎君ニヤル画手ハ、トッテ四マーラ 又ーオバーチャンガ行ッタ中
見セテ下サイ 又一作バーチャンヲ太郎君様ニ字ガヨメナンダラウ・・・］

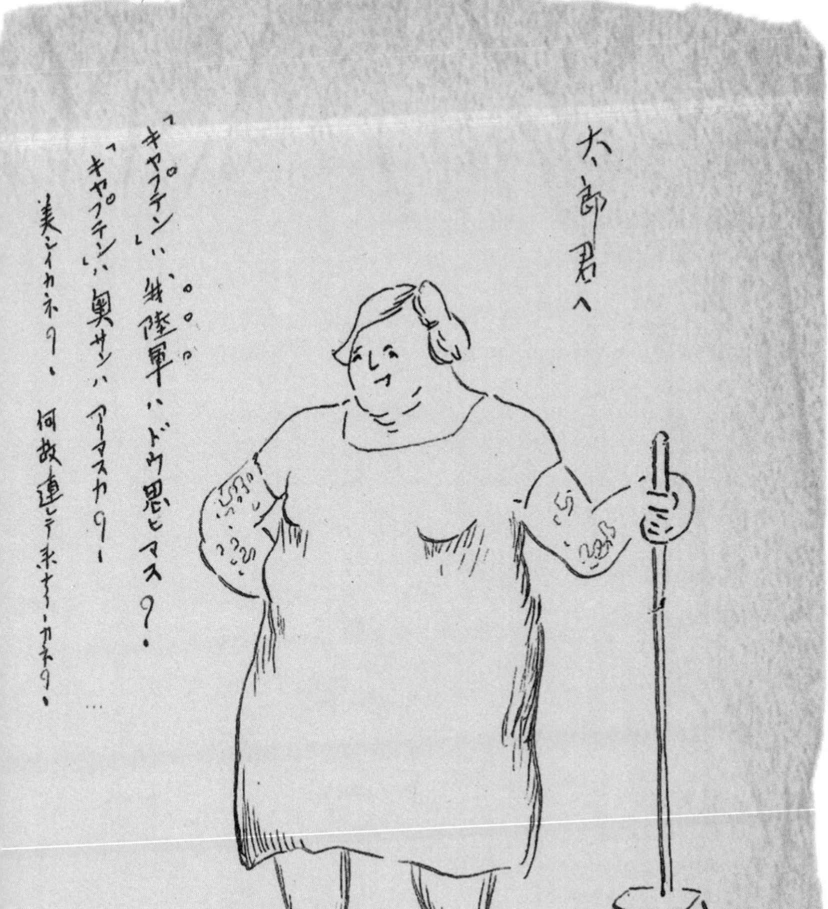

太郎君へ

「キャプテン、、、、、、、、。
「キャプテン、、我陸軍ハドウ思ヒマス？。

「キャプテン、、奥サン、、アリマスカ？ー
美シイカネ？、

何故連レテ来ナーイカネ？、
、、、

御父サンヨリ

Captain, so what do you think of our army?

Captain, are you married?

Is she pretty? Why didn't you bring her with you?

What? You say you have kids? Wow, two of them, huh…

My husband's a corporal in the army. He's a good-looking fella too.

We don't have kids…

What do I weigh? About one hundred and twenty kilos.

This? I had this tattoo done when I was young.

This job? Yeah, I've been cleaning houses for military personnel for exactly thirty years now.

What's Japan like?

You know, I happen to be a great dancer.

I was even better when I was young.

(She is quite emphatic about this.)

Your father is talking to his new maid, an elderly woman built like a sumo wrestler. The woman's husband is a non-commissioned officer who is in my regiment.

(Be sure to save the letters I send to Taro and show them to Grandmother when she comes from Kake [Kuribayashi's native village] to visit. Like Taro, she doesn't read.)

Your father thinks to himself:
"She's like a character out of a cartoon. She has her hair neatly parted at the side... Boy, she talks non-stop. But this is just fine with me...I can practice my English on her and kill time as well."

MUCH BETTER THAN THE BUSES BACK HOME

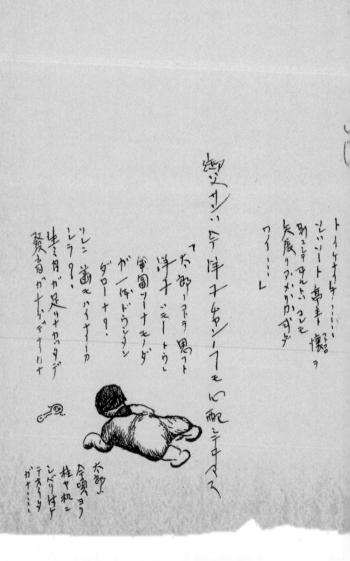

女中ノ御姿サンガ此處 自動車ヲ買ヒ換ヘタ云フノデ
御父サンニ見セテ居マス

ナルホド
コレハ〱
丁寧ニ渡
ツクラ大郎
気持ヨー
ゼ〲……

キャプテンヨ
ワタレヤ 自動車ヲ買ヒ換ヘタヨ
四百ドルサ、古トシテ、柏場モノサ
歩ハ、カオ〱ター アレハ 高主ヤハダロ

高主ト駛市、別ニコテ卆ネ
高主ハ、ホント〱、人ダガ酒ヲ
飲ムリ、バタケ〱アルデ何時モ
私ハ金ヲ ホダルデ困ル
今年ニナツテ居ルモノ
確ガ 貧ラキ、ベラ〱メ〱

父サン 腹、中デ思ヘラク
「コンナ渡ノ自動車デモ
日本ノ田舎ヘ歩ツテナル程
自動車マリ 乗ツ程イ〱ア」
ホント〱日本デ ドーカシナイ

MUCH BETTER THAN THE BUSES BACK HOME

My maid is showing me her new car.

Very nice, very nice.
If you drive it carefully, it'll last you a long time…

Captain, I have a new car. It cost me $400. I got
a pretty good deal on it, for a used car.
The other car? I gave it to my husband.

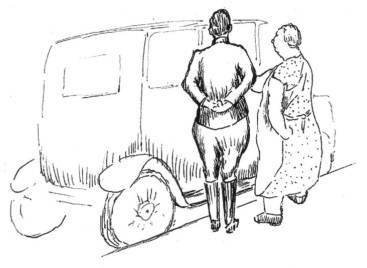

My husband and I have separate accounts.
God knows, he's a really good man, but he drinks and gambles like
there's no tomorrow.
He's always pestering me for money.
I don't know how much I handed over to him this year…
Blah, blah, blah, blah…

Your father thinks to himself:
"This old woman's car looks better than the buses running around in
the Japanese countryside. Japan has to do something about that."
Even so, only in America would a husband and wife have separate
accounts.

Your father is a little anxious about Yoko-chan.
If I remember correctly, Taro was already crawling around at her age.
I wonder what's wrong.

And no teeth yet?
She was premature—could it be she's slow developing?

When Taro was her age, we had to tie him up to a desk or a pole...

I BOUGHT A FLASHLIGHT: September 25, to Taro, from Father in Ft. Riley, Kansas

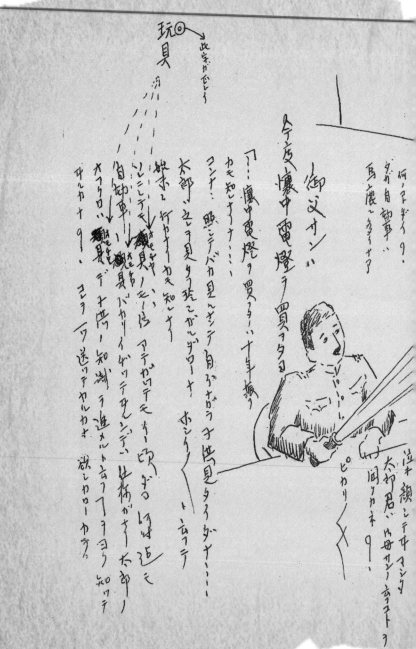

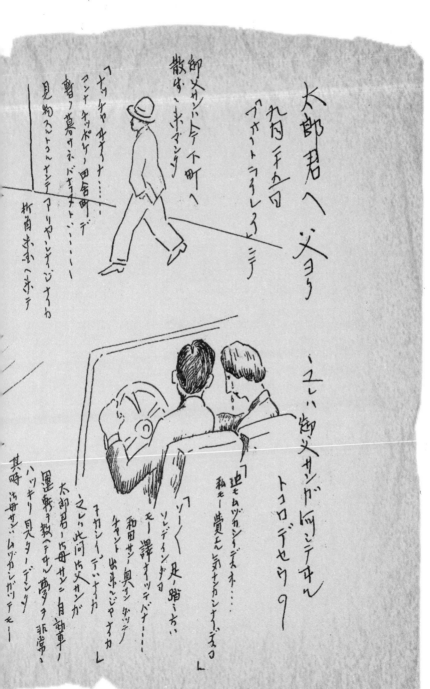

Your father is taking a walk downtown.

"Now what am I doing in this godforsaken place...
There's nothing worth seeing.
After coming all the way to America, I get stuck in a place
like this.
I can't believe the number of cars."

Guess what your father is doing in this drawing.

"This is too hard...I am ready to give up."

"Good, good. Your foot is in the right place. There you
go...
Even Mrs. Wada can do it."
Isn't it funny? I had a dream the other day, quite clearly as a
matter of fact, that I was teaching your mother how to
drive...
Your mother was finding it so difficult, she was ready to cry.
Are you minding your mother?

I BOUGHT A FLASHLIGHT: September 25, to Taro,
from Father in Ft. Riley, Kansas

Your father bought a flashlight.
It's been ten years since I had one.
I am like a child flicking it on and off.
Taro will love it and probably won't let go of it.
We may be in trouble here.
Come to think of it, Taro is at the age when he can have one.

He can't be playing with toy cars all of the time.
Does Taro's mother know that toys stimulate a child's cognitive
development?
I think Taro will like this...I must send him one.

Shine—

Military attaché at the Japanese Legation in Canada

Kuribayashi returned from his studies in the U.S. in July 1930 and was appointed military attaché for the Japanese Legation in Canada in September of the following year. Thus, Kuribayashi's boyhood dream of becoming a diplomat was fulfilled.

Air Force captain Takashi Aoki, on his way to his post at the Japanese Embassy in the U.S., happened to be on the same ship as Kuribayashi. He recollects, "Kuribayashi was extremely knowledgeable about American affairs and his company made my voyage most enjoyable. After about a week, we arrived in Honolulu and were told of the bomb explosion at Ryujoko. 'We will be met in America with a cold shoulder,' Kuribayashi lamented. 'We are arriving at a bad time.' The Ryujoko explosion brought on the Manchurian Incident. The U.S. notified both China and Japan in January 1932 that it was not happy with the state of affairs in Manchuria. The relationship between Japan and the U.S. became tense.

Kuribayashi was with the Japanese Legation in Ottawa for two years. He seemed to enjoy a good relationship with the then-Minister of the Legation, Iemasa Tokugawa, a direct descendant of the Shogun.

His letters from Canada have not been found. But considering his ready pen, he was sure to have written frequently to his family. No doubt, he was free to have his wife accompany him, but Kuribayashi decided to relocate alone. In his letter (page 120), Kuribayashi says apprehensively: "If I bring the wife, I'd be worried about my children's education...No, I don't think a post overseas would be a good idea." He probably weighed his own ambitions against the importance of providing his children with a good education, and decided that the latter was of more concern. In any event, the world situation worsened from here on and Kuribayashi never took an assignment overseas again.

— To Taro —

I BOUGHT A FLASHLIGHT: September 25, to Taro, from Father in Ft. Riley, Kansas

I BOUGHT A FLASHLIGHT: September 25, to Taro, from Father in Ft. Riley, Kansas

There are many couples in the dining hall where I take my meals. This means we dine with many women.

Yipes!

Taro, you will know what I mean when you go overseas.

Minding his manners, your father stands like a true gentleman.

Inwardly, he mutters:

"It makes no sense to me. Why do men have to stop eating and stand every time a woman comes in? The wife walks in arrogantly and the husband timidly follows from behind. Hah!"

Driving along country roads alone is your father's favorite pastime.

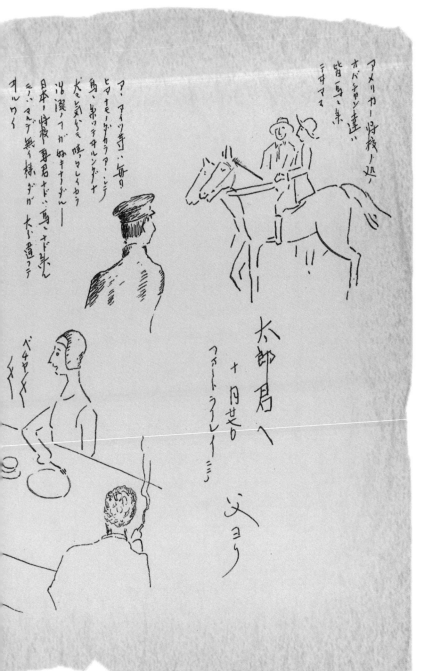

アメリカノ将校ノ処ニ
オベチャン達ハ
皆ノ家ニ来テ
デスママ

ア、アイツ等ハ毎リ
ヒマナモノダカラフト、ト
馬、ポッテオルンダナ
犬々気ガシテ、鳴々シクナラ
沼選ノフガ好キナガラー
日本ノ将校ヤドハ馬、ヤド来ヒ
ソシハ、マルデ無イ様ガイ大ニ通ッテ
オルワイ

太郎君へ

十月廿日
フォート ララレー ニテ

父ヨリ

Ladies married to American officers are always
riding horses.

Yes, they have a lot of time on their hands, so
they ride.
Of course, they are lively people so I imagine
they like to keep active.
I doubt any wives of Japanese officers ride.
Different circumstances.

This is your father at dinner.
It is absolutely amazing how much people talk here.
Of course, people should chat during meals.
In Japan, we are probably too quiet.
You are a chatterbox, Taro. Do you chatter while you eat?
Your mother is a typical Japanese woman, the silent type.
Is she teaching you to be like her?
Is this corn? Potatoes again, and beans too.
How can they feed you the same thing over and over?
Compared to this, the Japanese eat well.

"Oh my, you say the Japanese don't eat corn at meals?
You say potatoes are only for the poor?
Oh, I must say, you have developed a good sense of humor..."
(They think your father is joking.)

ISN'T YOKO BETTER YET?: October 27, to Taro, from Father in Ft. Riley, Kansas

ソレニシテモ太郎君ノオ母サンハ此頃マダ手紙ヲ
中々ヨコサナイナア・・・・寒サニ向ツテ
洋子ガマダ悪イノカナ9、弱イツテカラ
今月中ハ只一度ダケノタヨリヽツテ「ハ何カ変ツタコトガ
アルトカモ知レナイ」
「ヽマレハ
御父サンガオホンホンシテ
井ルトコロ デス
室内ハ何時モ暖カダカラ毛布ヲ
チョウト御腹ノ上ニ乗セテ井ルダケ
デス
日曜日ノ外ハ毎朝七時ニ起キナケレバ
ナラナイノデ閉口ダヨ
ソーデナイト朝飯ヲ食ヒハグレテ
シマウノデタマラナイ
然シ朝起キハイイヨ
太郎君ハ朝起キヲヤルカネ の、
朝ネ坊ヲシテハイケナイヨ

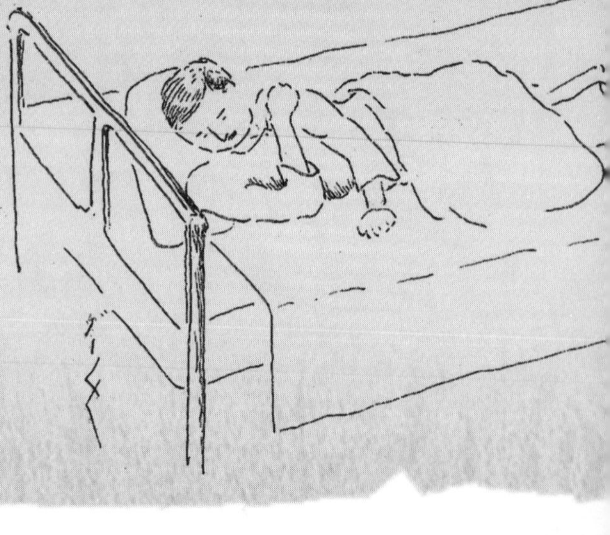

太郎君へ 十月廿七日 「オイトラレー」ニ於テ 父ヨリ

御父サンガ 一生県命勉強シテヰルトコロ

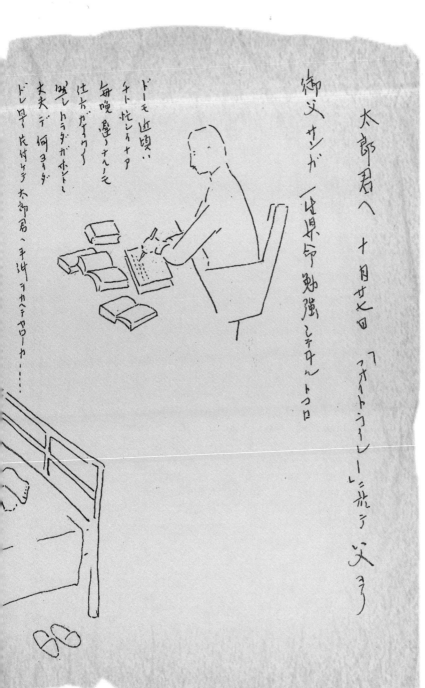

ドーモ 近頃ハ
チト忙シイナア
毎晩 遅クナンゾ
仕方ガナイワイ
シカシ トラダガホント
大夫デ 何ヨリダ
ドレ早ク片付ケテ 太郎君ヘ手紙ヲカイテヤローカ……

163

ISN'T YOKO BETTER YET?: October 27, to Taro,
from Father in Ft. Riley, Kansas

This shows your father studying hard.

I have been a little busy these days. To make up for it, I'm
up until late every night.
It's a good thing I have a strong disposition.
Let me finish up quickly and write a letter to Taro...
Come to think of it, I haven't heard from Taro's mother
for quite some time...
Is the cold weather affecting Yoko?
I understand she is not strong.
I've gotten only one letter this month and it has me
slightly anxious.

This is your father in bed.

My room is always warm so a blanket over my stomach is
sufficient.
I hate getting up at seven every day of the week, except
Sunday.
I miss breakfast if I'm late.
But rising early is a good thing.
Do you get up early, Taro?
Don't oversleep, now.

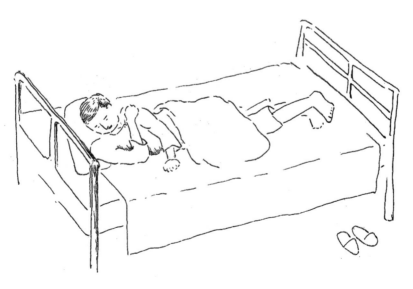

文、いちぇサン、いゃヲ考ヘテ呑ハイデセゥ9、

日本酒一升ビン十月半タノシメタガビン酒ニハモー
モー一合ヲ残ッテサナイ、ダカラソレヲ二合モヲカワ
跳々暮シ更ニモー四ヶ月跳ヲ杯トヲレ、デモ
エンゲイ、イリヲ呑テタラモ
今暫ク我慢ステ和部君。
、お誕生日一合ヲ分シ様ナ
コレヲテモ大リホニヤカラ
醤油ハ来ハ。
カンカン詰ニ買ッテ
ドーヱ我慢ニ来京
崇ボレナ…。

「ソシテコレヲ一年棒ダ」

「日本へ恰テカヲ酒ヲ呑ムカ 比頃ノーヲ
懐ィ出スヲ 酒二頭ヲ下ゲルダ〜十……
酒許リジャナイ お醤油三 頭ヲ下ゲカニ一鏡話ヲモ頭どんダ〜ヲ 呪友……

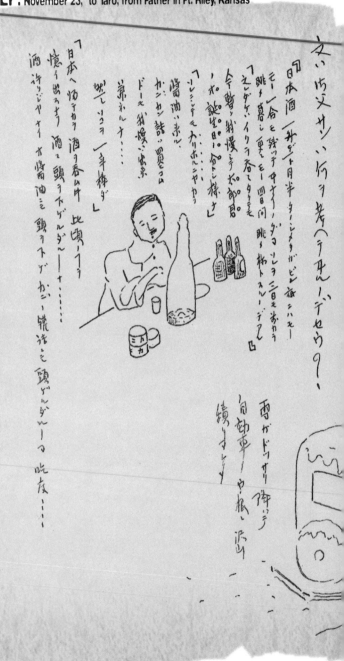

雪ガドッサリ降ッタ
自動車ハや根ニ限い出シ

鏡ネネネ

太郎君へ　十月二十日　「オートラーレ」ニテ

御父サン体操ヲシテヰマス

外ハ雪ガ家ノ中、夏ハ全部ガ

矢ニチルト日本ノ

ミダメノ冬ノ

生活ノ全

供スル

オイ、ハ、ニ、

モー犬ガヤツタカラ止スト

シ称カ

太郎ハ体操ヲヤルカナ？

MAKING A BOTTLE OF SAKE LAST FOR A MONTH AND A HALF: November 23, to Taro, from Father in Ft. Riley, Kansas

Your father is exercising.

It's snowing outside but it's
as warm as summertime
inside the house.
When winter comes, I think
of the miserable winters in
Japan.

One, two, one, two.
I've had enough exercise, so
I'll stop for now.
Do you exercise, Taro?

It snowed very heavily and fresh
snowdrifts cover the roof of my car.

Can you guess what is going through your father's mind in this drawing?

"I made this bottle of Japanese sake last for a month and a half, and now there's only a single goh [0.16 liters] left. I have been staring at it for three days now and plan to keep staring at it for four more days."
"I am determined to save it until your birthday, Taro."
On the other hand, I've had soy sauce sent from California and stored up on canned crabs.
This is too much to bear...
Nope, I'm going to wait.

When I return to Japan, I am sure I will think back on this experience and bow my head in thanks to sake. And not only to sake, but to soy sauce and even to canned crab...

太郎君へ 十二月九日

ネ、トラシレーデ 父より

オ父サンガ来、寒ッ晩
自動車ノ樽関節ヲ凍ミ割シレヲ
レ、ンマッタトコロ ナンダヨ

「ヤヤヤ……遂々ヤッチャッタ」…
コリヤドーモ デカイ横ッ骨ダ
百ドル位デ済メバイ、ガナ
早ク五寸出シテ マンマールヲ
サンテ置ケバ コンナコトハ
ナカッタニナ
ホント シャクダナ……

コレタ処ハ 太郎君ノ知ッテ
ヰルアウイヨーレ、中ナシダヨ

THE ENGINE OF MY CAR FROZE OVER AND CRACKED:
December 9, to Taro, from Father in Ft. Riley, Kansas

This is what happened to my engine one cold night. It froze over and cracked.

"Yikes...I can't believe it...
We've got extensive damage here.
Will $100 cover it?
I should have invested 50¢ for that alcohol and squirted some in, then this wouldn't have happened. How irritating..."

"Taro, the engine is the part of the car that gets hot.
Do you remember touching it and saying 'ouch!'?"

whoosh
whoosh

Even in freezing weather, your father keeps up his exercises.

Don't let the cold weather keep you indoors.
Walking is very good exercise...
Cold days always remind me of the days of hard training I endured as a young recruit...

Your father wears his yukata [cotton kimono] when he studies at night.

Hmm...this doesn't sound right.

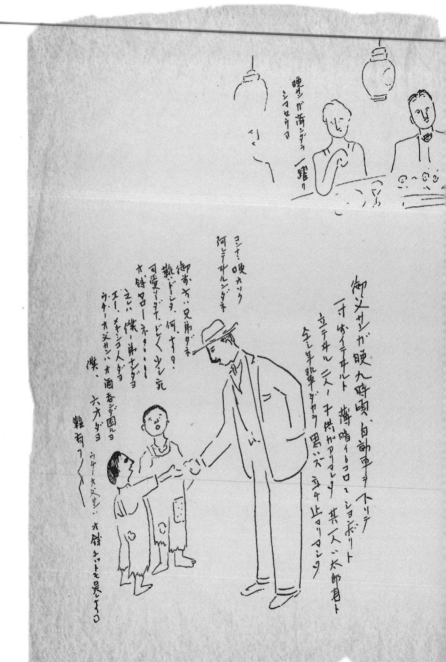

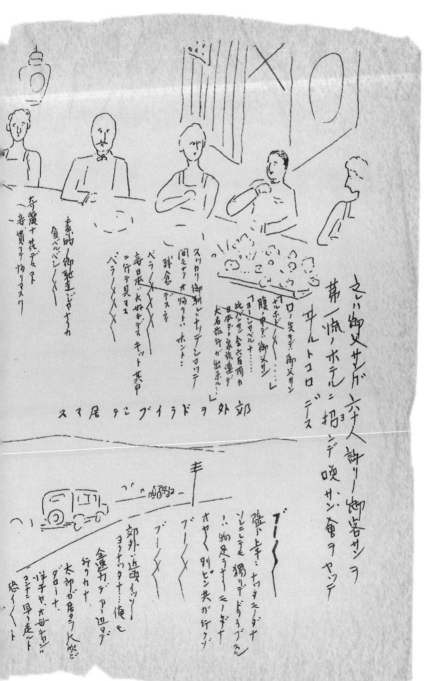

I FEEL LONELY DRIVING BY MYSELF

This is your father holding a banquet at a fancy hotel for about sixty guests.

"Yes, yes, of course," I am saying outwardly.
Inwardly I am thinking, "They never stop talking…"
This dinner is costing me a lot of money. In Japan, it would pay for a family vacation, first-class all the way.

"You've adjusted here so well.
We are sorry to see you leave.
Yakkity yak yak.
I just love Japan."

"I will surely visit you soon.
Yakkity yak yak."

"This is quite a feast.
Eat, eat, eat."

"Oh such lovely flowers.
I should like to take some home with me."

"We must take a twirl after dinner."

I am taking a drive in the suburbs.

Honk, honk, honk.
I've become quite a good driver.
But it's lonely driving all by myself.
Well, well…look at those pretty girls.

Honk, honk, honk.

The suburbs have gotten prettier…
I'm going to step on the gas—full speed ahead!

Taro would love this if he were here.
Yoko and her mother would squeal with fright.
Honk, honk, honk.

I FEEL LONELY DRIVING BY MYSELF

About nine in the evening, your father got out of the car and
walked a bit. There were two children standing sadly in the dusk.
One must have been Taro's age so I stopped.

"What are you doing out so late at night?
You're brothers, aren't you?
What happened to your shoes? What! No shoes?
What a pity. Here, let me give you some money…"

"This is my younger brother. Yes, we are Mexicans.
My father drinks a lot…unfortunately.
I'm six years old.
My father won't give us any money.
Thank you, thank you, thank you."

Kazunoko and Johnny Walker Red

Kuribayashi was greeted with laughter when he said that potatoes were only served in the homes of the poor in Japan (page 159). Surely, it would be hard for Japanese people to be served corn, potatoes, and beans at every meal. Upon his return to Washington, Kuribayashi devoured herring roe without even bothering to sit down (page 196). Kuribayashi had soy sauce sent from California, where there was a large Japanese population, and his craving for Japanese food seemed to intensify daily. "His favorites were sekihan (rice with red beans), kobumaki (seaweed roll), kazunoko (herring roe), and kyurimomi (pickled cucumber). In the Shinshu area, a whole herring would be wrapped and rolled in seaweed and cooked until very soft—so soft that chopsticks would go right through it. My mother cooked them every New Year," says Takako, the second daughter.

Kuribayashi writes about staring at what little was left in his sake bottle (page 167). Did he enjoy drinking? Takako says that "when it came to nightcaps, his drink of choice was Johnny Walker Red on the rocks. He did not drink too much sake."

Circa 1935, from their home in Setagaya, Kuribayashi would often take Takako with him to shop at Niko, a specialty store which handled imported food. When overseas, Kuribayashi dreamed of Japanese food and when in Japan, he cherished British whiskey. It certainly does seem as if "the Japanese eat well" (page 159). It is said that vegetables were sparse in Iwo Jima. Kuribayashi would chop up a basketful of eggplant and cucumbers into tiny pieces to distribute to his men—he took none for himself.

FINALLY ONLY FOUR MORE MONTHS TO GO:

December 23, to Taro, from Father during his 1,300-mile-trip back to Washington, D.C.

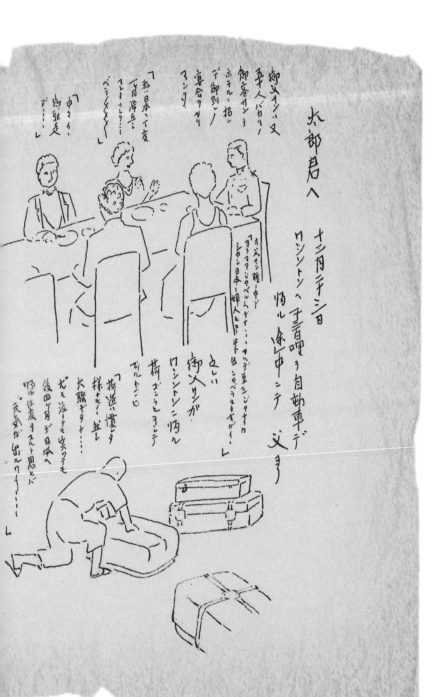

太郎君へ

十二月廿三日
ワシントンヘ子言喋ヲ自動車デ
歸ル途中ニテ　父ヨリ

御文ヲ又
五十人バカリノ
御客サンヲ
ホテルニ抱ン
デ御別レノ
宴會ヲヤリ
マシタ

「私ハ日本ノ友
ヲ首將兵ニ
マレマシテ……
ベラ メメ……」

「中々イイ
御馳走
デ——」

「オ父サン鶴ヨーナ
ヨウナワンジャベンダ……マルデ豆ニジャガカ
ション 日本一婦人ヲ……キ……ニ……シャベラールナスガイ……」

でんわかけて
椅子ゴシニコシテ
ワシントンニ歸ル
「様ニ慣レタ
様子ニ並ヒ
大韓ギタ十……
犬ヱ海ヲ笑ウテモ
後四ヶ月 デ日本ヱ
歸ル途毎……思ヒバ
元気ガ出ルワー……」

FINALLY ONLY FOUR MORE MONTHS TO GO:

December 23, to Taro, from Father during his 1,300-mile-trip back to Washington, D.C.

Your father again invited about fifty guests to his farewell banquet in a hotel.

"I spent a month in Japan. And..." Blah, blah, blah.

"This is a fine meal..."

Your father is thinking to himself, "She is such a talker...
Like a comedienne. Japanese women should talk about half as much."

Here is your father packing his bags to return to Washington.

I am used to packing by now, but it's still a hassle...
Whatever...I will be in Japan in four months.
The mere thought of that revives me.

This is your father bidding farewell
to his friends.

"Goodbye."
Goodbye. When you come next
time, be sure you bring your
family...
Yakkity, yak, yak.
When I have saved enough money, I
will go to Japan to view the cherry
blossoms.

Blah, blah, blah...

"Goodbye. Actually, I'm not too
keen on traveling overseas."

Here I am, heading straight to Washington.
However far you go, there is a sea of vast plains.

太郎君へ　一月二十五日　ワシントンミテヨリ

御父サン三百哩位ノ
アレガニー山脈ヲ
横断シテ
ススム

「父ヲ
大ク驚ロカナ
谷ガ深イゾ
ソロソロ行カヌト
大変ヲヲ

「ソレデモヤハク何ウ
山ガ重ナツテ
合ツテ
クルゾナ

ベロベロ…………
ベロベロ……

「ウオットライツ〜カラ
「ワシントンレヲデナ十三百哩
大ゲザニ雪道」デ非常ニ
危ナカツタ

「ウエストライン〜カラ
「ワシントンレヲデナ十三百哩
「ガッシャーン
「二度
トデロカックタリ　ブツカツレ
タリシテガ大ンナ損害
モナルデ　助カツタゾ

「ゾ！

CAR TROUBLE IN SNOW TO COMPLETE THE MISERY:
January 25, to Taro, from Father in Washington, D.C.

whoosh...

I am making my way through three hundred miles in the Allegheny Mountains.

The climb is steep and the valleys deep.
I must proceed cautiously or I will be in trouble.
And there are many mountainous roads still ahead.

It is 1,300 miles from Ft. Riley to Washington.
Most of the roads are covered with snow and are very treacherous.
I collided into something twice or something collided into me.
Bang! But nothing serious.

"Darn. Now what?"

Car trouble in a snowstorm to complete the misery.

A flat tire at a time like this.
This is serious.

This may take a few hours to fix and I won't make it
before dark.

Brrr, it's cold, cold, cold.

whoosh

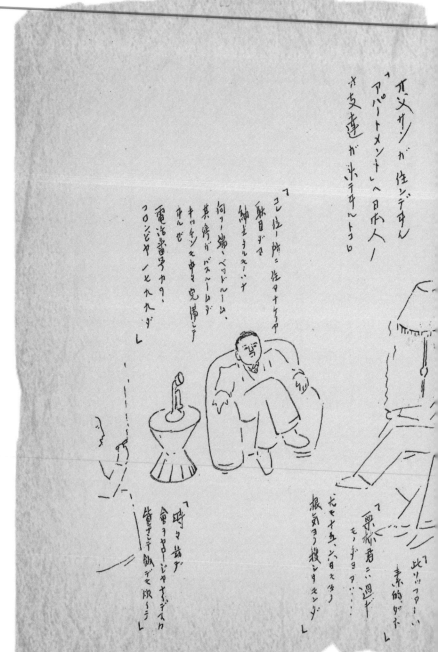

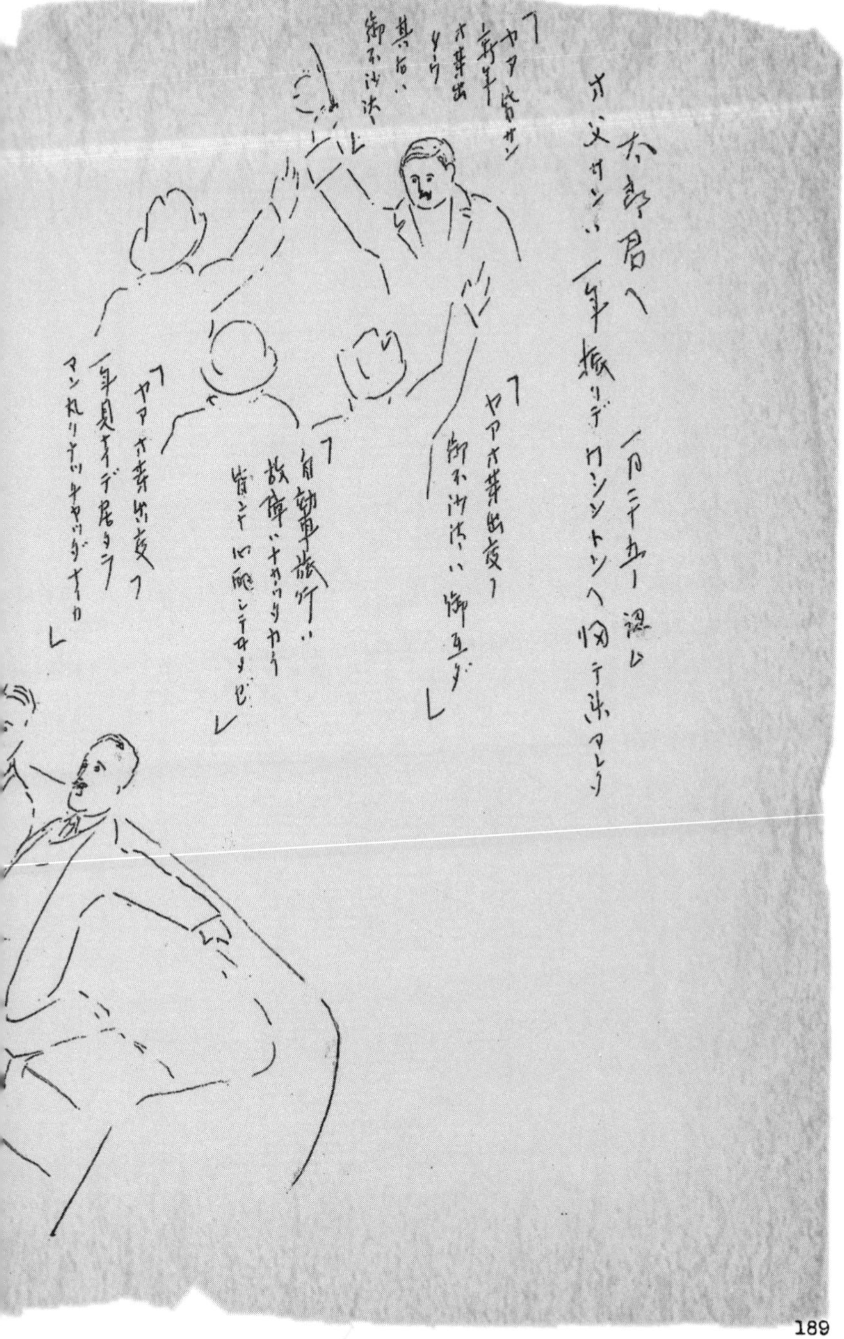

HAPPY NEW YEAR, TARO: To Taro, written on January 25

Your father has returned to Washington—it has been a year.

"Happy New Year everyone.
Sorry I haven't been in touch."

"Happy New Year.
Long time no see…"

"Did you have any trouble on your way over? You had us worried."

"Oh, Happy New Year. You've put on some weight since we last saw you."

Here are some of my Japanese friends visiting my apartment.
A gentleman deserves to live like this.
Over there is the bedroom, and you have the bathroom next to it.
Your kitchen comes with all the frills.
Your phone number? It's Columbia 1799.

You've got a nice sofa here.

You don't deserve such a nice sofa, Mr. Kuribayashi.
Ha ha ha!
"Of course, it took him over two weeks to find it."

"Let's use this place for our get-togethers.
We can cook some rice."

— To Taro —

IF OUR WIVES SAW US NOW: February 4, to Taro, from Father in Washington, D.C.

太郎君へ　　二月四ヶ　「ワシントン」ニテ　父ョリ

えゝ×文サン、アパートへ
オ友達ガョッテ来テ
皆ンデ二テ日本ヲ食ウ
ニテ・夕
ニテ喰べ様ト
シテセルトコロ
デース

「コレハ所ヲ爆共、
見セタラ何ト
思ッデローナ
「違カ扁通ヘ
ニテャ飯ヲ
「四置ケロ
「女ニ生レテ
ヨカッタ…
コンドハ
毎日ノレテ
コンナ頭ニサレー
「一毎ラクレト
オレハウ女ケンテモー
リコ……

IF OUR WIVES SAW US NOW: February 4, to Taro,
from Father in Washington, D.C.

Here you see some friends gathered in your father's apartment preparing a Japanese meal.

"If our wives saw us now, what would they think?"

"Somebody take a picture."

"Good thing we weren't born women; we'd have to do this sort of thing day in and day out."

"That's why women don't develop intellectually. Their chores don't require brains."

"No, no. They do use their heads. They have to plan meals for the day and think back on what they served the day before...

"That's nothing..."

"Hey I smell rice burning."

"Don't worry. I turned down the gas."

Here are some Western children at play in the snow.

Cheers!

Get out of my way!

Here I come.

— To Taro —

DEVOURING KAZUNOKO: March 4, to Taro, from Father in Washington, D.C.

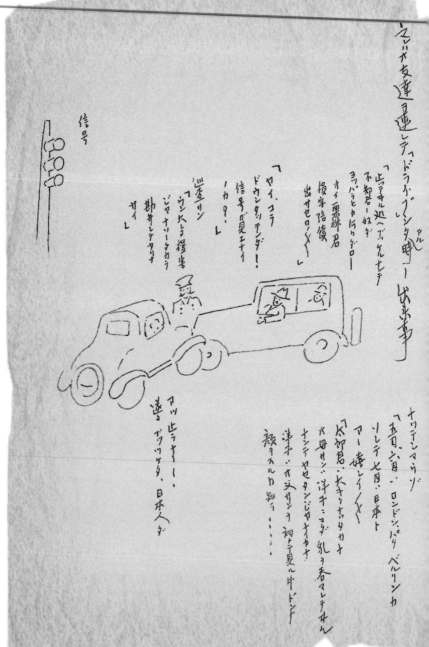

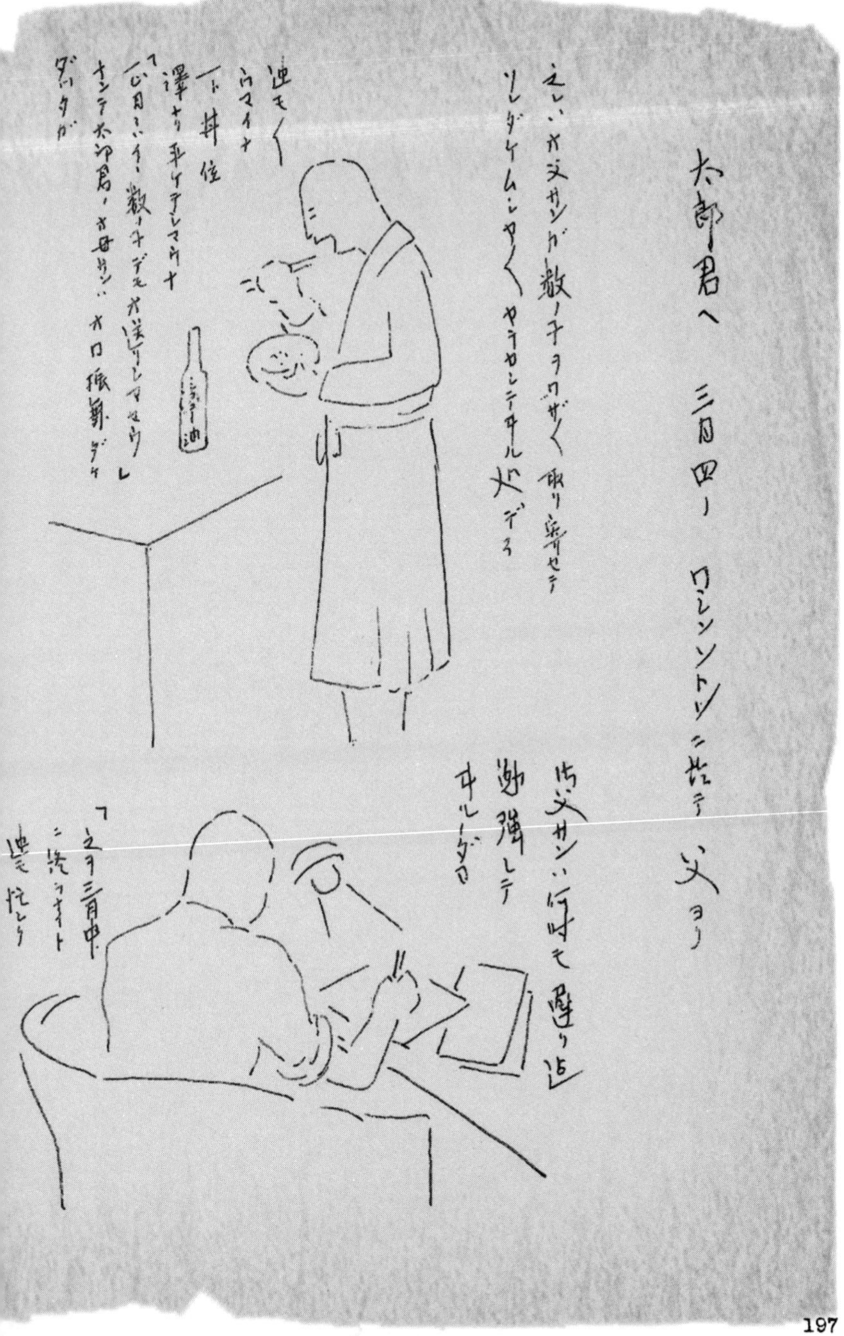

太郎君へ　三月四ノ　ワシントンニ来テ　父ヨリ

えゝ、お父サンガ　赤ン子ヲロザク　取リ宛セテ
ソレダケムニャ〜　ヤラヤシテ井ル　丸デゝ

お父サンハ　何時モ　壁ニ近リ
勉強シテ　井ルンダ

「えゝ三月中　ニ渡ッテト　思フカラ」

迪キ〜
ハマイナ
下宿住

「沢リ　平ケテアリマスカ
〇月ニテ　数字デモ　お送リシテオクリ
ナンテ　お父君、お母サンニ　オロ振動ダイ
ダイタカ

DEVOURING KAZUNOKO: March 4, to Taro, from Father in Washington, D.C.

This is your father devouring kazunoko
[herring roe].
I had it sent special delivery.

It is very, very tasty.
I can polish off a bowlful in no time.
"I will send you some good herring roe at
New Year's," your mother said.
Apparently it was just lip service.

This is something that happened when I took a drive
with a friend.

"This is an outrage. I can't believe he ran into us
when we were stopping at a light.
He's probably been drinking.
Kuribayashi, make him pay for damages.
Make him pay, make him pay."

Stoplight

"Hey ! What were you thinking!
Didn't you see the traffic lights?"

Policeman: "There really isn't too much damage done.
Why don't we let him off."

Uh-oh, we didn't stop in time.
It was an accident. They're
Japanese.

— To Taro —

DEVOURING KAZUNOKO: March 4, to Taro, from Father in Washington, D.C.

Your father always studies until late at night.

"If I don't get this done by the end of March, I'll never finish it.
Come May and June, I'll be in London, Paris, and Berlin. And I'll be in Japan by July.
Oh this is wonderful.
Has Taro grown?
I wonder if Mother has lost weight breast-feeding Yoko.
I wonder what kind of face Yoko will make when she sees her father for the first time…"

About Tadamichi Kuribayashi's family

After graduating from the Army University, Kuribayashi was married on December 8, 1923. That would be the same day Japan would attack Pearl Harbor in 1941 (Japanese time). His bride was nineteen years old, thirteen years younger than the groom. Her name was Yoshii Kuribayashi (no relation) and she was from an old family from his hometown. Their first son, Taro, was born in November of the following year when the couple was living in Tokyo.

Kuribayashi's fondness for Taro is apparent from the illustrated letters that were sent to cover the geographical distance between father and son. Kuribayashi became more of a disciplinarian toward Taro as the years passed, perhaps because Taro was his heir. The first daughter Yoko was born in 1928, and the second daughter Takako was born in 1934. It is to these two girls that Kuribayashi shows his gentler side. This change is reflected in his communications from Iwo Jima. To his young wife, perhaps because of their great difference in age, Kuribayashi proved to be a considerate husband until his final days.

His career as a soldier separated father from children and husband from wife, and it was probably to fill this gap that Kuribayashi continued to write his stream of letters.

After being notified of her husband's death, Yoshii suffered from typhoid fever. Her own mother and Yoko succeeded in nursing Yoshii back to health, only to die themselves, one after the other. Their residence in Tokyo was burned down in an air raid. After the war, Yoshii and the children picked up their lives in Tokyo. Although she had never worked a day in her life, Yoshii found employment and managed to raise Taro and Takako. When the Ogasawara Islands were reverted back to Japan in June 1968, Yoshii dreamt of a smiling Kuribayashi saying, "I am finally back in Japan."

THE TWO YEARS PASSED LIKE A DREAM: To Taro, from Father, sailing across the Atlantic on the S.S. Laconia (on the fourth day of the voyage when I have time on my hands)

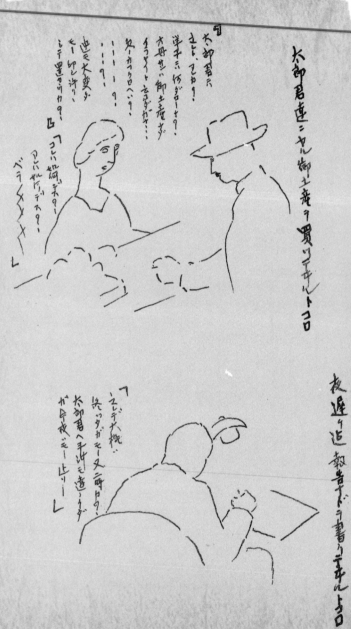

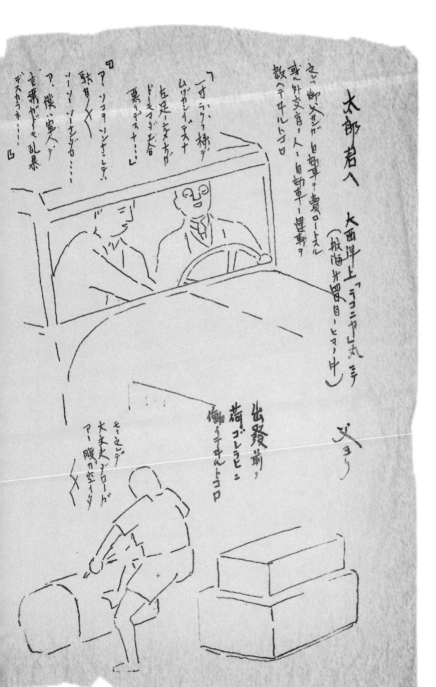

THE TWO YEARS PASSED LIKE A DREAM: To Taro, from Father,
sailing across the Atlantic on the S.S. Laconia (on the fourth day of the voyage when I have time on my hands)

Here is your father teaching a diplomat, to whom he will sell his car, how to drive.

"It's not as easy as it seemed. My left foot needs work..."

"Oh, no, no, no.
Yeah, that's more like it...
Sorry, sir, my military training has made me a little abrupt."

Here I am packing my bags.

I think I'm about done here. I'm feeling very, very hungry.

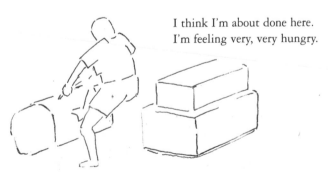

Here I am buying gifts to take
home to you.

I wonder if Taro would like this.
How about this for Yoko?
Your mother insists she doesn't
want anything...
What about my mother in Kake?
...?
...?
This is beyond me.

Maybe I'll just get a few token
gifts.

"May I help you, sir?
Would you like to see that one?
Yakkity, yak, yak..."

Here I am filling in my report
late at night.

"This is about it. Oh, it's already
two a.m.
I haven't written to Taro for a
while.
But I'm calling it a night."

之ハ際ニ自動車ヲ賣リ捌キテ、

長々間來リマシタガ自動車ニ大別レヲ告ゲル）トコロ

ロ、ソレジヤ御別レデス
ドージキス御用ハ
ナスツテ ゲガなど ナサ
ヌ様ニネ‥‥

「御丈夫デ・大批レ
トコロ数ヘテ頂リテ
ボトン前御レマス」

THE TWO YEARS PASSED LIKE A DREAM

Here I am bidding farewell to the car, which faithfully served me during my years here.

"Well, so this is it.
Please drive carefully
and take care, now."

"Thank you for taking the time off to teach me
how to drive."

I wonder if you understand, Taro. I am aboard a train, taking leave of Washington.

The two years passed like a dream.

THE TWO YEARS PASSED LIKE A DREAM

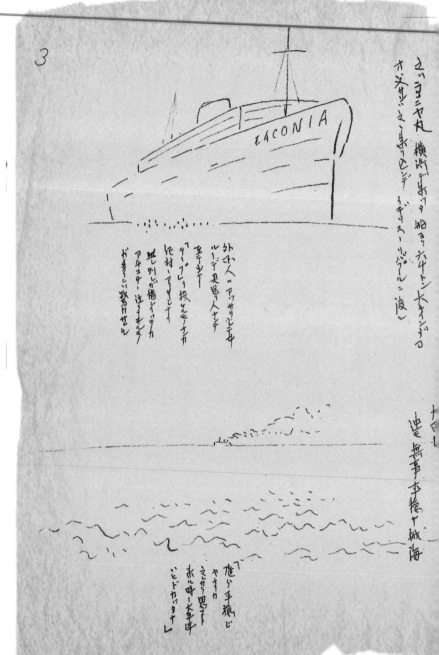

210

文ユリ本部君三　想像　モッカナイ　話ダネ

高ク　ビルヂング　許リ　ギッシリ　五寸モンデ十二　ニョーク　下町　ブロードウェー　ヤンヂロ

谷様・様ト道・楽　ブロク　練固モ・並デ走ツてますに・い　自動車、

とてれい　身体を出れ　て　経・人出トロ　ヤンヂロ　画ヨリ　カケナ・ネ、　道・両側・　辞・様ミタ・ク

当父も　き　此ムラガ・や、　そんヂ様　其か　糀ミタッテ・・・

此車ラ不・欠不様連ガ　{縦横無尽へ走ッテ}

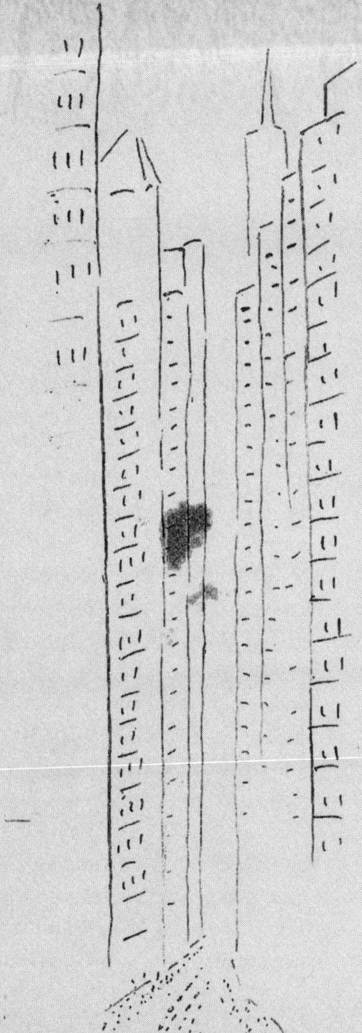

THE TWO YEARS PASSED LIKE A DREAM

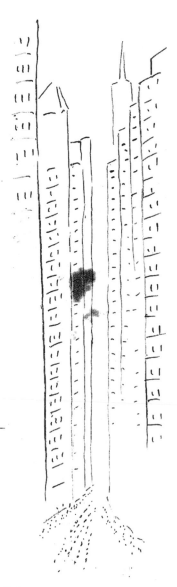

This is something I know Taro will have trouble imagining.

This is a place called Broadway, an area in downtown New York, crammed with high-rise buildings. Cars make their way, bumper to bumper, through the valleys running below the buildings.

What looks like a family of ants crawling on the south of the street, are actually a crowd of people. I can't even begin to draw it for you.
Your father is actually among them but you won't be able to find me. And crisscrossing the area under these streets is the subway system.

This is the S.S. Laconia. It's about six thousand tons
heavier than the ship I boarded at Yokohama.
Your father is sailing on this ship headed to Liverpool,
England.

Foreigners are not very sentimental, so not many
people are seeing the ship off.
Nobody throws ribbons.
However, I'm surprised at the number of people
crying—maybe they're finding it hard to say goodbye.

THE TWO YEARS PASSED LIKE A DREAM

Crossing the Atlantic.
It is smooth sailing.

"The seas are calm.
Compared to this, the trip over the Pacific
was very choppy."

TO TAKO-CHAN
From June 1944 to January 1945 (from Iwo Jima)

At the age of fifty-four, Lt. Gen. Tadamichi Kuribayashi took up his post as the army's Commanding Officer on the island of Iwo Jima. He addressed the following letters to his second daughter, Takako, who had been evacuated alone from Tokyo to her mother's family home in the country.

The letters reveal Kuribayashi's tender feelings toward his young daughter, with whom he was able to spend very little time.

June 25, 1944

To Tako-chan.

How are you Tako-chan?

I can still picture you and your mother as you stood at the gate of our home, seeing me off.

And I often dream of my going home and taking you and your mother into town. But the dream will have to wait.

Tako-chan, my hope is that you will grow up quickly so that your mother can rely on your help.

Please take care, study hard and mind your mother so that I will have peace of mind.

Farewell.

From Father in the battlefield

September 20, 1944

Tako-chan!

The letter I posted on September 14 reached you on September 19. I am amazed at the speed.

I am keeping well and am glad that you too are in good spirits.

I feel much better knowing you are getting along with your cousins, Mie-chan and Katchan [Note 1], who live with you. You are the baby of the family and have always depended on your mother. This may have led you to be a little self-centered. It may hinder you from making friends, especially when you start school. Try to give this some thought.

You tell me that your grandmother offers prayers for me every morning. That may be why I am in good health. However, this is a very big war and I am not certain that I will be able to return home safely. My heart goes out to you Tako-chan. If I do not make it home, please mind your mother and grow into a healthy young woman. It will give me great comfort.

Unlike the nice cool weather in the countryside that you mentioned, the heat here is unbearable. But Fujita-san [an aide] seems to sleep very well [Note 2], judging from his snoring. I sleep well, but incidentally, do not snore. Sometimes, a soldier on duty will talk in his sleep and wake me up. Snoring and talking in one's sleep are not good because they disturb others.

We hear air raids day and night and they are quite horrifying. Tokyo may be raided soon, but you are safe in the countryside so don't you worry.

Your mother says you are not writing to her often enough. Please try to do so more often, this will put her fears at rest.

This is all for today. Goodbye. Take care.

From Father in the battlefield

To Takako-san.

Yes, as you indicated, I used 'hi' instead of 'i' in 'omoi.'
And in return, I will correct the mistakes in your kanji [characters].
In 'sleep', the correct kanji is 'nemuru.'
It is 'tabemono', not 'dabemono.'
You used the wrong character for 'shin' in 'shinsetsu.'
The correct kanji for mitomu is ——
The correct kanji for kangaete is ——

November 17,1944

Tako-chan! How are you? I am doing well.

We had two air raids last night; the first one immediately after I went to bed, the second one around midnight. But your father had an interesting dream.

It went something like this: You came out of your bath whimpering, so I asked, "Why are you crying? Was the bathwater too hot for you?"
Your mother laughed and said, "I have a feeling she just wants something sweet," and she started to breast-feed you. The two of you lay down and you began to happily suck on her breasts, your cheeks ballooning out. Then your older sister came along and poked at your cheeks saying, "Tako-chan is too old to be nursing. I can't believe this!" That is all, but I saw all of your faces so clearly, I felt I was there with you. How about that? Interesting dream, don't you think?

There have been frequent air raids recently. Japan herself will most likely be attacked. But you are in a safe place, so not to worry.

It's still sweltering here, but it must be getting cold in Japan—in Shinshu, especially.

Tako-chan! The chill in Shinshu cannot be compared to that of Tokyo, so you'll have to be extra careful not to catch a cold. Bundle up tight. If you crawl under a kotatsu [fireplace with a coverlet] to nap, chances are you'll catch cold, so I do not recommend it. Also, I remember napping in a kotatsu when I was very young and burning my toes badly. You must take care that nothing like that happens to you.

Tako-chan, do you have any cavities? You mustn't forget to brush regularly. If you don't brush, your teeth will decay and cause you much pain.

Do you get stomachaches? If you ever have diarrhea, it's best you don't eat too much.

Well then, bye-bye. Please write to your mother from time to time.

From Father in the battlefield

To Tako-chan.

How are you? I am fine and working hard.

Your letter dated November 14 got to me seven days later. Your writing is very good but let me indicate two errors in the kanji that you used: 'inaka' and 'shinsetsu.' And you used the word 'totemo' [very] a total of six times. It is better not to keep repeating the same word.

I don't remember sending you my photograph, so I am guessing that the person who took the picture sent it to you.

A person from the navy press crew came to shoot some footage of me. He tells me it may be released in a newsreel. And today, a photographer from the Army Press Corps came to snap many photos of me. He has informed me that they will be sent to your mother so ask her to show them to you.

As you requested, I have done a few self-portraits. I will draw more in my free time and send them to you, okay?

Tako-chan, our hen has just hatched four chicks. A soldier on duty put seven eggs in her nest to warm, and four of them have hatched today and are chirping away. We keep ten birds outside. Insects are all they have to eat, but they have grown quite large.

Tako-chan! It must be getting cold in the country by now. Be careful not to catch cold. It's still hot over here. Mosquitoes and flies buzz everywhere.

I'll say goodbye for now. Bye-bye.

I received a letter from your uncle today, but haven't had the chance to reply.

Please give him my regards.

From Father in the battlefield

December 23, 1944

To Tako-chan.

Are you well, Tako-chan? Your father is fine. It must be freezing over by your way.

It has cooled down here somewhat, but we are still in our short-sleeved summer uniforms. The trees and grass are still green and the flies and the mosquitoes are as bad as in the summer.

I know there are no air raids where you live, so I am not worried. But Tokyo is being bombed and I am concerned about your mother's safety. Over here, we are routinely bombed once during the day and twice at night. But we are safe in our bomb shelters.

Tako-chan, it ended with just the four chicks the other day. We tried to hatch all seven eggs, but one went bad and we heard some chirping inside the other two, but we neglected to help them out, so they died the next day. The four chicks are very active and playfully follow the mother hen around, pecking around for insects. They are only three days old but there is already sibling rivalry. Our hens often lay eggs but unfortunately for us, they lay them in the grass, not in their nests.

The officer on duty found sixteen eggs in the grass the other day, but they were all rotten. It was a pity. Tako-chan, I had a dream about you recently. You had grown very tall and were almost my size. You were wearing the trousers I gave you and had bobbed hair. I was standing in amazement, taking in your height, when your mother came along. The two of us proceeded to try to pick you up and swing you around like in the old times, but you were too heavy for us.

Tako-chan, do you still wear those trousers I handed down to you? Have they gotten too short for you? I know Sadaoka-san [the tailor] is not there so you can't get them adjusted [Note 3].

Tako-chan, take care you don't catch cold this winter. A little extra attention can keep you from catching a cold. I am always careful, so I never come down with colds, or anything else for that matter, and am always ready to work.

I will say goodbye for now. Take care and stay well. Please say hello to Grandmother, Grandfather, Uncle, Auntie, Toshinori-san [Note 4] and everyone else.

From Father

January 18, 1945

To Tako-chan.

How are you doing? I am fine.

Your mother wrote the other day, informing me that you had made straight A's in school. It has made me very happy. Keep up the good work and try to get straight A's always. Try to remember though, that getting good grades in a school in the country doesn't necessarily guarantee good grades in a school in Tokyo. Therefore, never be arrogant or stop trying. Another important thing is to stay physically strong and to be the kind of person everyone likes.

Academic excellence alone will not win you friends. You must be considerate to others and never be mean or sarcastic. This is very important to remember as you grow older; especially for young women. It is my hope that you will stay in good health and become someone who is liked by all.

Tazoe-san [Note 5] was able to visit Tokyo the other day; no doubt, his father must have been very happy to see him. I myself cannot leave. The fighting is only becoming worse and I fear I may not be able to return alive. If that should be the case, please mind your mother, grow up as fast as you can and avenge my death.

Goodbye, then. Stay well and don't catch cold.

From Father

January 28, 1945

To Tako-chan.

The letter dated January 6 was written very well.

I had no idea you were familiar with all those difficult words. 'Active,' 'fiends,' 'charging spirit,' 'annihilate,' 'advance,' 'home front'...
Do you actually understand what all these words mean? If you do, you've certainly grown very wise and I am very happy.

Just let me point out five errors in your kanji: 'kichiku' [fiends], 'semeyosete' [assault], 'gekimetsu' [annihilate], 'kushu' [air raid], and 'shintai' [body].

Even where I am, the mornings and evenings are getting quite cool. But I am still in my summer clothes, the grass and the trees are still very green and the flies and mosquitoes are still a nuisance.

The enemy air raids are getting fiercer. Sometimes, the night raids number ten. At times, we are bombed by battleships. But your father and his soldiers are all well and fighting.

I'm comforted by the thought that there are no raids on your area, but it must be very cold. Please stay healthy. Are you wearing my trousers that Sadaoka-san altered for you?

I will bid farewell for today. Please stay well and study hard and strive to become a person who is liked by all. Goodbye.

From Father

P.S. The four chicks that were hatched only two months ago have grown very big. They walk around with their mother pecking for food. But the other day, they managed to break the ————, which I took a lot of trouble to make.

Notes

Page 217
Note 1: Mie-chan and Katchan - Takako's cousins, the older brother of Yoshii and Tomomi Kuribayashi's children.
Note 2: Fujita-san - The lieutenant taking care of Kuribayashi's affairs.

Page 221
Note 3: Sadaoka-san - The tailor that Kuribayashi was friends with. He now lives in Kochi [prefecture].

Page 222
Note 4: Toshinori-san - Takako's cousin, the older brother of Yoshii and Tomomi Kuribayashi's oldest son.

Page 223
Note 5: Tazoe-san - Takako's classmate from Matsubara Elementary School in Tokyo. His father was also at the battle front in Iwo Jima.

How the illustrated letters came to be released

Matsushiro-cho, Nagano City in Nagano Prefecture, is known as the area where the Sanada clan built its castle. There is also an underground shelter there that was dug during World War II for the purpose of transferring the Imperial Headquarters and the main government agencies. The shelter extended nearly six kilometers, and near the entrance was a privately operated reference library called Jidai no Yakata (Period House). Since Tadamichi Kuribayashi was born in Matsushiro, many of his belongings were exhibited there, including a few of his illustrated letters.

The editor of this book visited this museum in the autumn of 2000. Impressed by the quality of the pictures he saw, he made the decision to publish them in a book. Incidentally, the library was closed down at the end of that year. About a year later, the editor heard rumors that Shogakukan Paperbacks was interested in publishing significant materials pertaining to this particular era. The editor took this as a sign and started his search for the illustrated letters.

The editor learned that Kuribayashi's son, Taro, to whom the letters were addressed, made his home in Tokyo. Taro had the letters carefully filed. And considering the passing of years, they had been very well preserved. These picture letters had been evacuated from the Kuribayashi household in Tokyo (later burned down in an air raid) to the home of Mrs. Kuribayashi's parents in Nagano and saved.

Preserved along with the letters were photographs and letters sent from Iwo Jima which are also included in this book. The editor cannot help but wonder why nobody had thought to publish them before. Taro and other members of the Kuribayashi family readily agreed to the request that the letters and photographs be made into a book.

TO MY WIFE AND CHILDREN

From June 25, 1944 to February 3, 1945 (from Iwo Jima)

Of the forty-one letters Kuribayashi wrote to his wife and children from Iwo Jima, the first and last letters contained such candid information that it is believed the only reason they passed censorship was because of Kuribayashi's standing.

On March 17, 1945, Kuribayashi wired his farewell message to the headquarters of the Imperial Army and faced the full-scale attack mounted by the Americans eight days later. He died in action on March 26.

June 25, 1944

Greetings. I trust you are all well.

I, too, am keeping well. I am in a horrible place that does not even compare to Baotou and Guangdong. It is hotter here than Guangdong. In the five days to a week that I have been here, I have been badly sunburned and my skin has peeled off many times. The heat is so oppressive that one is drenched in sweat and the clothes on one's back are always uncomfortably soaking wet.

There is no spring water here, so we must do with rainwater. I long for a glass of cold water but nothing can be done. The number of flies and mosquitoes is appalling. There are no newspapers, no radios and no shops. There are a few local farms, but no shelter suitable for anything other than livestock. Our soldiers pitch tents or crawl into caves. The caves are stuffy and the heat and humidity are intolerable.

I, of course, endure similar living conditions. I sleep alongside Makita, my aide. We still have plenty of food, but must be resigned to eating the same things every day. Fruit, including bananas, was said to be plentiful, but in truth, there is none. We do not have sugar, either.

I can only describe it as living in a cave in the middle of a barren plain like Sugadaira in Shinshu. It is a living hell and I have never experienced anything remotely like it in my entire life.

The enemy line is closing in and the officers and soldiers are very tense. We have already experienced three air raids and are under heavy bombing from firebombs and strafing from machine guns. On the sixteenth, a large bomb exploded near our air raid shelter and I was blown away with it. Luckily, I escaped without a scratch. All we can do during these air raids is to hold our breaths and pray. The air raids come without any warning so we are always on our toes. We often find ourselves eating rice balls inside the shelter. Our meals are very irregular; we eat breakfast at ten, lunch at eleven and dinner at sixteen hours. (Tokyo will be bombed any day soon. You must prepare to run if you are to survive. It is important that you take only what is precious. Keep some water and food that will not spoil with you at all times. Firebombs can rain down from the sky and envelop Setagaya in a sea of flames. Please be ready.)

Up until now, it is thought that enemy air raids have been largely experimental. They will soon begin a full-scale attack and bombs will be dropped day and night, non-stop. In addition, our soldiers and officers are monitoring and guarding our shores, around the clock, to prevent troops from landing on our shores. Even I must rise at three-thirty or four.

If this island falls into enemy hands, the land of Japan will be bombed day and night without respite. We take our responsibility seriously. We are all prepared to lay down our lives. I fear that my chances for survival are less than one percent. The battle is raging right before our eyes. With the exception of the times that I am overcome by fatigue and am asleep, my head is filled with battle scenes and honorable deaths and thoughts about the future of my wife and children.

I was at the point in my life when I was ready to make my family happy, as a husband and father, when this enormous war erupted and I was assigned to protect this strategic island. So be it—this is my duty. Judging from my health, I would have enjoyed another twenty years or more and would have engaged in many kinds of work. Now because of the fiendish American military, I must succumb to these difficulties. You may find it hard to accept my fate, like the ———— family (although they may have been just acting out the part). But please try to accept it as destiny and live your lives to the fullest.

So as not to curb morale, I doubt any official announcements will be made to the public regarding air raids or enemy landings. But it is a fact that this alarming situation will continue and bombings will become even more frequent.

Please give some serious consideration to evacuating right away. The local people remaining on this island run and hide behind rocks each time there is an air raid—the women and children are deathly afraid. You must ask your older brother for advice on your evacuation. An adjutant in the Tokyo Division can help you make preparations to transport freight.

If this island falls into enemy hands, there is no use worrying about the children's schooling. Taro is one thing, but Yoko should take a leave of absence or transfer to Nagano High School. Stay together as a family as much as possible. It may be good to keep the maid until the evacuation; you will need help in an emergency.

Please do not expect further communication from me. (Although if there is a venue, I will write again.)

To my children—my final wish is that you mind your mother, support and help her. Encourage each other and stay well. Taro, I am praying that you have grown into a strong young man and that you are worthy of your mother and sisters' trust. Yoko is a solid young girl so I do not worry. Your mother is a shy woman and my heart goes out to her. Tako-chan, I regret that my time with you was short. Please take care of yourselves and grow into fine adults.

To my wife and children
Farewell from your husband, your father

P.S.
1. With this delivery, I am sending back some items I brought with me but which are no longer necessary. They may also serve as mementos (you will probably not receive any of my belongings or my ashes). If a military courier arrives, I may have more items to send back. Please do not send any more care packages, whiskey included. You never know whether packages will make it here and even in the event that they are safely delivered, I may no longer be alive to receive them.

2. I think I tended to most of my household duties, but I regret I did not attend to the draft coming through the kitchen floor. I believe Taro took care of the things I entrusted him with. Has Hayashi returned yet?

3. I have not been in communication with anyone recently. If any of my former friends or soldiers ask after me, just inform them that I am at war somewhere in the southern quarter.

[**Note**: The following text was written in the margins] This letter is for your eyes only. Please do not talk about its contents with anybody.

February 3, 1945

I have not heard from you for twenty-four to twenty-five days, but I trust all is well.

This is the coldest season so I worry that someone is suffering from a cold. How are plans for the evacuation coming along? Are you still thinking of sending our things to Kofu while the family sticks it out in Tokyo?

As I mentioned before, the enemy will step up their air raids around springtime and so I would recommend that you move while you can, to a safe place.

I doubt that you will actually have a bomb dropped on you, but I worry that you may be harmed by the fire caused by the firebombs. Here, they are dropped regularly. And although there is nothing more to burn on this island, we still go up in flames. (They simultaneously drop drum cans full of gasoline to create a sea of fire...I doubt they could do this to Tokyo.)

In spite of this heavy bombing, I am keeping well. We are desperate for vegetables and have started to clear some land. Perhaps this work agrees with me. I am in even better health and I believe I have gained some weight. I notice this when I take the occasional bath.

This environment is not conducive to good health and we have many who are sick among us. Almost everyone has fallen ill at least once, so I feel fortunate that I have been the exception.

Today, Major Omoto, a high-ranking adjutant, is making a liaison trip to Tokyo and I am asking him to carry this letter back to you. However, please do not entrust Otomo with anything for me. As I've said before, I need nothing.

Please take good care of yourselves. Don't catch cold and try to stay well. If you feel tired, I recommend a good massage.

Don't let Taro oversleep in the mornings or steal a nap in the kotatsu. Have him keep his wits about him at all times and practice self-discipline.

I must stop now as the plane is leaving. Goodbye.

Emergency cable dispatched at 5:00 hours, March 17, 1945-Classified

1. The war is in the final stages.
2. Our corps will launch an all-out assault tonight (March 17) in order to destroy the enemy.
3. All units will attack the enemy at midnight, fighting to the last man. We will not look back.
4. I will be at the head of the company, in front of every soldier.

Lieutenant General Kuribayashi

Note
Some time later, Colonel Tanemura, a member of the Imperial Headquarters, handed this cable to the Kuribayashi family, saying "please consider this his remains."

Farewell wire from Commander Kuribayashi, 24:00 hours, March 17, 1945

The war has reached the final stages. Ever since the beginning of the onslaught, my men have fought with courage that would have brought even demons to tears. They have fought against the unimaginable superiority of enemy weapons that attacked from land, sky and sea, using their bare hands and fists. I am in debt to them.

However, the enemy attacks know no end and our men have fallen one after another. We have let this strategic post fall into enemy hands. I regret this deeply and sincerely and I hereby extend my profound apologies. All bullets have been fired, not a drop of water is left. As we prepare to stage the final battle, we are reminded of the grace of our emperor and we have no regrets facing our end, our bodies and bones torn asunder to become dust. Until this island is returned to us, the Imperial land is not safe and therefore, even as spirits, we will lead the attack to make this island ours once again. As I bid my farewell, I single-mindedly pray and hope with my entire being that Imperial Japan will emerge victorious and secure.

I am confident that the officers and soldiers on the island of Chichijima and Hahajima will prevail and destroy the enemy. Please relay my message to them.

Finally, I leave this humble poem and ask you to humor me by reading it.

> *Sadness overcomes me as I am unable to fulfill my duty for my country,*
> *Bullets and arrows are no more*
> *I, while falling in the field without revenge,*
> *Will be reborn seven times to take up my sword again.*
> *When ugly weeds run riot over this island,*
> *My heart and soul will be with the fate of the Imperial nation.*

Notes
Page 228
Note 1: Baotou and Guangdong - Baotou is now a city located in the autonomous region of Mongolia located in the People's Republic of China, Guangdong is now Guangzhou.

Page 228
Note 2: Setagaya - The Kuribayashi family home was located in Matsubara in the Setagaya ward of Tokyo.

Battle of Iwo Jima

By Shigetoki Hosoki
(military historian and former army captain, the 55th class of the Army Officers Academy)

Iwo Jima, which is the southernmost territory of Japan, is located midway between Saipan and Tokyo. Because of its strategic location, this small island with the smell of sulfur was transformed into the site of a hellish battle. The island had three airstrips and was an indispensable base for defending mainland Japan. Of course, that meant this island would also prove to be a tactically advantageous airbase for the American military. America needed to take this island to facilitate her bombing of Japan with its B29 bombers. Iwo Jima was eight kilometers long and four kilometers across. At its narrowest point, it was a mere eight hundred meters wide. Cliffs jutted out one hundred meters above the surface of the sea for most of the shoreline. But there were sandy beaches to the south and west of the island, making it easy prey for enemy landings. On the southern tip of the island rose Mt. Suribachi, a volcano with an altitude of one hundred and sixty one meters. To the north of the mountain was a plateau of rugged terrain; ranges of low mountains, Tamayama, Nidan-Iwa, and Osakayama rose to meet it. Kuribayashi built strongholds in these mountains and succeeded in holding off the enemy's northward march for over a month.

On June 19, 1944, as the Americans were landing on Saipan, Kuribayashi, the new Commander of the Corps stepped down on Chidori airstrip on Iwo Jima. His company, the 109th Corps, was comprised of mostly middle-aged and older soldiers, and they were carrying out orders to dig trenches along the water's edge. Kuribayashi made a careful survey of the island and put a stop to the digging of the trenches and ordered his men to retreat inland. His strategy was to utilize the rugged features of the terrain to make strongholds. This decision was in direct defiance of orders from his superior in Saipan, Commander Obata of the 31st Division. Including his stint as military attaché at the Japanese Legation in Canada, Kuribayashi had spent a total of five years in North America, and it was perhaps this experience which made pitting half-naked Japanese soldiers on the beach against American bombardment a totally unacceptable idea to him. Hirohide Iwatsubo, now ninety-three years old, worked under Kuribayashi as Chief of Staff. He recalls that Kuribayashi often said, "America's productive powers are beyond our imagination. Japan has started a war with a formidable enemy and we must brace ourselves accordingly." (As recounted to the writer in February, 2000.)

Saipan, where men fought heroically at the waters' edge, fell to the Americans on July 7, 1944, a day on which Japanese traditionally celebrated the Festival of the Stars. This defeat put a large dent in the confidence of the Tojo cabinet.

On June 15, five days after Kuribayashi arrived on Iwo Jima, the Americans began their air raids on the island. By July 4, America had control over the air space. Dodging these air raids, the Japanese kept digging trenches ten meters underground and secured caves. On July 1, Kuribayashi's group became the Ogasawara Corps (operations encompassing the islands of Iwo Jima, Chichijima and Hahajima), and was directly under the command of Imperial Headquarters. Kuribayashi was assigned as the Commander of the Corps. He was a rationalist and as a commander, a bit of a loner. When Joichiro Sanda, Imperial Headquarters' Chief of Strategy, came to inspect Iwo Jima, Kuribayashi commented that "the most gratifying thing was being given a fine group of twenty-five executive officers from the Infantry School. Under the new leaders, soldiers, who were previously dawdling under aged platoon leaders, have begun to respond energetically to orders. The graduates of the Academy's 53rd class are to be commended." On the other hand, Kuribayashi's blunt remark that "should the enemy attack us now, we shouldn't last more than a week or ten days," is a matter of public record. A former member of Kuribayashi's staff, who survived because he was acting as a liaison officer and in Tokyo at the time of defeat, said of his superior, "Kuribayashi was outspoken and self-assured to the point of being arrogant. I often wondered how he could hold such ironclad beliefs." The more mild-mannered of his men found his forceful style unbearable. The Chief of Staff was replaced by Tadashi Takaishi, an expert on infantry battles, and Kenji Nakane, a strategist. The new Brigade Commander was Yoshiki Senda.

As an individual, Kuribayashi was a very warmhearted man. He wrote: "It must be destiny that we as a family must face this. Please be convinced as such and stand tall with the children at your side. I will be with you always" (September 5, 1944). "I regret that I must close my life in this godforsaken place because of the Americans, but I will defend this island until the last moment and pray that Tokyo will not be bombed" (September 12, 1944). Apparently, he opened up his heart to his family. Takeo Abe, who came back alive and devoted the remainder of his life to retrieving the ashes of his fellow soldiers, writes, "By the end of 1944, we were forced to save rations for battle and we foraged around for edible weeds. Suffering from chronic diarrhea, empty stomachs and lack of water, we dug bunkers in the sand under a merciless sun and constructed underground shelters that were steamy with heat. We used salt water, lukewarm from a well on the beach, for cooking, and saved what little rainwater we could for drinking. But one water-bottle a day of water was the most we ever had to drink."

On February 19, 1945, American troops made their first landing on the southern shore of Iwo Jima. On the 23rd, they took Mount Suribachi on the southern tip of the island and raised the Stars and Stripes.

This writer was stunned to find the following comments in the "Iwo Jima Association Report," a collection of memoirs by Iwo Jima survivors. "The men we saw weighed no more than thirty kilos and did not look human. Nonetheless, these emaciated soldiers who looked like they came from Mars faced the enemy with a force that could not be believed. I sensed a high morale." Even under such circumstances, the underground shelters that the Japanese built proved advantageous for a while. Enemy mortar and bombing could not reach them ten meters under the ground. It was then that the Americans started to dig holes and pour yellow phosphorus gas into the ground. Their infantry was also burning its way through passages, slowly but surely, at a rate of ten meters per hour. A telegram has been preserved that says, "This is like killing cockroaches." American troops made daily advances to the north. On the evening of March 16, they reported that they had completely occupied the island of Iwo Jima. Twenty-four hours later, the Japanese army led by Kuribayashi was surrounded in a small area (seven hundred meters long, two hundred to seven hundred meters across). On this day, Japanese newspapers published Kuribayashi's telegram along with his poem. In its editorial, the *Asahi Shimbun* urged the Japanese people "to learn from the bravery displayed on Iwo Jima and follow suit."

However, even after that, Kuribayashi doggedly persisted and did not stage a banzai attack. He died in the early hours of March 26, thirty-five days after the Americans landed (February 19, 1945). According to records in the Defense Agency's historical archives, 20,933 soldiers fought on Iwo Jima, and a total of 1,033 survived. On the American side, three divisions of Marines made the assault, and 6,821 died and 21,865 were injured, making a total of 28,686 casualties. Navy Lt. Gen. Holland Smith recollected that, "In the Battle of Iwo Jima, the aggressors suffered more casualties than the defenders. At the end, combat operations were running at less than fifty percent."

U.S.-occupied Iwo Jima was the site for 2,400 emergency landings for B29 bombers on their way back from bombing Tokyo—it saved the lives of 27,000 crew members.

Today (as of Japanese first edition, April, 2002) Mrs. Yoshii Kuribayashi is nearly one hundred years old and still well. Her husband's sword rests behind her in an alcove in his memory. The war hero continues to protect his family.

By Koichi Edagawa (non-fiction writer)

Tadamichi Kuribayashi, who later became Lieutenant General of the Japanese army, returned to Tokyo via Europe from America in July 1930. He was forty years old. A month later, in August, President Herbert Hoover appointed Douglas MacArthur (age forty-nine) as Army Chief of Staff. MacArthur was the youngest appointee for this position in the history of the American military.

Fifteen years later, in 1945, the destinies of these two military men were clearly divided.

Kuribayashi defended Iwo Jima for six months, fighting against the fierce American onslaught, and ultimately died in action. This eventually led to the final stage of the war between Japan and America. When the atomic bombs were dropped on Hiroshima and Nagasaki, Japan unconditionally surrendered to the Allied Forces. Arriving in Japan as Supreme Commander of the Occupation was, of course, Gen. Douglas MacArthur.

The contrast between the fates of the Japanese commanding officer who died on the sands of Iwo Jima and the American hero who reigned supreme in war-scarred Japan is obvious. Perhaps, this makes the gentle illustrated letters that Kuribayashi sent to his young son even more poignant.

In 1929, while Kuribayashi was in the U.S., the country experienced the Great Depression brought about by the crash of stock prices in the New York Stock Exchange. The following ten years were a difficult period in America, but these illustrated letters did not reflect any of it.

Perhaps it was because the letters were addressed to a child, but it could also be due to the fact that Kuribayashi was a military man. He was within the military system, a unique group that exists, protected as it were, from general society.

At the beginning of the Depression, veterans who were having financial difficulties demanded early payment of their pensions. They gathered to demonstrate in Washington and set up camp around Congress. It was MacArthur who led an infantry detachment to disperse the group. The adjutant at the time was Maj. Dwight Eisenhower, who in time became an American president.

This operation is an example of the role that the military plays. The general public did not approve of the tactic, however, and it was thought to be a contributing factor to Hoover's losing his bid for re-election to Franklin D. Roosevelt.

Kuribayashi was an elite member of the Japanese army and as such, he was on the same side of the fence as MacArthur and Eisenhower. Thus he was not in a position to be attuned to the economic turmoil around him. The people depicted in his letters are military personnel and their families, a landlady, a maid and at times, children he saw on the street. Businessmen and laborers, the mainstays of capitalism, do not appear at all. However, Kuribayashi, who wanted to be a journalist or a diplomat, may have inadvertently cut to the core of American culture without being swayed by political and economic issues. This is apparent in his recognition of the automobile.

Cars appear constantly in his drawings and writing. His obsession is shown in his purchase of the newest model, the Chevrolet K. One cannot help but smile when reading the passage where he dreams about teaching his wife how to drive, only to have her start to cry.

It is noteworthy that he often mentions the pleasure he derives from driving. In a letter written from an army base in Kansas, a state in the Midwest, he confesses to his son that his favorite pastime is driving alone on a country road.

Americans embraced the automobile in the 1920s. A law was passed in 1921 that authorized federal, not state, governments to regulate the construction of roads. It was around this time that roadside gas stations became familiar sights and motels were built to provide travelers with lodging.

Kuribayashi drove 1,200 miles from Kansas to Washington, D.C. at the end of 1929. It was only a short time after the road connecting the Midwest to the east coast was paved. He was, no doubt, one of the very few Japanese who chose this mode of travel in the U.S. at that time.

The availability of cars also allowed Americans to experience their own country firsthand. Even now, as it was then, the best way to discover America is not to set down roots in a big city like New York, but to embark on an endless road trip across the country. The neverending roads, the scenery, the people-watching—it all adds up to a true picture of what America really looks like.

Through his drives, Kuribayashi must have physically experienced this vast nation. When driving through the Midwest, he commented that "there are wide open spaces everywhere. Compared to this, Japan is pitiful." And when his maid shows him her car, Kuribayashi muses, "This old woman's car looks better than the buses running around the Japanese countryside. Japan has to do something about that."

Much later, the officer lamented how badly Japan was underestimating America's power of production (page 240). The sheer size of America and the power of the vehicles that conquer that space...

When being pummeled by the overpowering enemy in Iwo Jima, did fond recollections of the drives through the countryside drift through Kuribayashi's mind?

While gazing at the drawings and reading the letters, one cannot but feel that something is wrong. One begins to realize that the drawings and captions do not face each other.

The letters were meant for his young son, Taro, but the drawings were not drawn from Kuribayashi's point of view. Instead, he was the object in his drawings and the composition was such that the artist was someone else. That someone is his son. Kuribayashi drew as if Taro was looking at him, and therefore, Kuribayashi himself is in the pictures.

Kuribayashi may have been using a multifaceted approach in his drawings— in other words, he is his son and his son is himself. His letters contained lessons he wanted to teach his son. On the other hand, he depicted scenes from his day through his son's eyes. Running through his mind were the words, "If that young boy of mine were here now, what would he see?" This is an expression of love for his family. As he drives, he thinks, "Taro would love this. Yoko (a daughter born after Kuribayashi left for America) and Mother would squeal with fright. Honk, honk, honk." The honking of the horn speaks for him.

Taro was too young to read. Thus his father decided to write illustrated letters. The letters sent from America were read by the boy's mother who showed him the pictures. Therefore, the young child was receiving letters from both father and mother and making an emotional connection at the same time.

Today, these picture letters would be defined as being interactive. Father, mother, and son are all recipients and senders of these letters. A virtual situation is created. The father borrows the son's eyes and talks to his wife; the wife listens to her absent husband and talks to her son. The son certainly must have felt the strong presence of his absent father along with that of his mother sitting beside him.

Nurturing a child with love and watching him develop was perhaps the one great joy in Japanese households at that time. These picture-letters represent one man's desperate efforts to preserve such an ideal.

Ten years pass and the same man confesses in a letter to his family that "I was at the point in my life when I was ready to make my family happy," but he must give it up. He talks of his decision to "succumb to these difficulties," and encourages his family to try to "accept it as destiny and live your lives to the fullest."

It would be wrong to dismiss this as just another war story.

CHRONOLOGY of the life and times of Tadamichi Kuribayashi

1891	Tadamichi is born on July 7, the second son of Tsurujiro Kuribayashi and wife Moto in Kakeku, Saijou, Matsushiro-cho, Hanishina-gun, Nagano Prefecture (presently known as Matsushiro-cho, Nagano City) (Ohtsu Incident)
1894	(Start of Sino-Japanese War)
1898	Tadamichi enrolls in Hoei Elementary School in Hanishina-gun, Nagano Prefecture
1902	Graduates from Elementary School. Enters Matsushiro Higher Grade School
1904	(Start of Russo-Japanese War)
1906	Graduates from Matsushiro Higher Grade School. Enters Nagano Prefecture Middle School (currently Nagano High School)
1907	Studies shakuhachi (bamboo flute)
1911	Applies to and is accepted at Army Officers Academy and Shanghai Toa Dobun Shoin. Graduates from Nagano Prefecture High School December - Joins Narashino Cavalry 15th Regiment as a cadet
1912	December - Enrolls in the Army Officers Academy in Ichigaya, Tokyo (26th class)

1914	May - Graduates from the Academy and is assigned to the 15th Cavalry Regiment. Is made Second Lieutenant, army cavalry.
	(Start of World War I)
1915	December - Enrolls in Army Cavalry School, Otsu Branch, majoring in equestrian art
1916	November - Graduates from Army Cavalry School
1918	July - Made Lieutenant, cavalry
1920	December - Enrolls in Army University (35th class)
1922	Death of younger brother
1923	August - Is promoted to Captain
	November - Graduates from Army University with honors; receives a sword from the emperor
	December 8 - Is married to Yoshii (nineteen years old)
	December - Assigned to Narashino 15th Calvary Company Commander
	Moves to Narashino, Chiba Prefecture
	(Great Kanto Earthquake)
1924	November 27 - First son Taro is born

1925	May - Assigned to Cavalry Group

1928	March - Departs to study in the U.S. on S.S. Taiyomaru, via Hawaii and San Francisco to Washington, D.C.

May - Settles in Boston (Cambridge, near Harvard University)

August - Secludes himself from fellow Japanese, in an American home in Buffalo, to perfect his English

November - Returns to Washington, Japanese Embassy

November - First daughter Yoko is born in Tokyo

1929	January - Moves to Ft. Bliss near El Paso, Texas Purchases Chevrolet

Makes the acquaintance of Captain Weitman

Attends emperor's birthday celebration held by Japanese community

May - Acts as guide to military attaché to Mexico Lieutenant Colonel Shikeri Takeshita and his wife on inspection tour of El Paso

August - Travels to Mexico (invited to Minister Arata Aoki's reception, reunites with Major and Mrs. Yoshio Wada)

September - Moves to Ft. Riley, Kansas

December - Holds farewell parties prior to his departure

Drives solo from Ft. Riley, over the snowbound Allegheny Mountains, to Washington, D.C.

October - The Great Depression. New York Stock Exchange crashes

1930	New Year's in Washington, D.C.

February - Receives orders to return to Japan

March - Promoted to Major

April - Assigned Military Affairs officer. Leaves Washington, D.C. and boards S.S. Laconia in New York City bound for Liverpool, England for an inspection tour of London, Paris, Berlin

July - Arrives in Japan via Siberia. Makes his home in Taishido, Setagaya-ku, Tokyo

1931	September - Attaché to staff headquarters

Appointed military attaché to the Japanese Legation in Canada (the first military attaché)

(The Manchurian Incident)

1932	(The 5.15 Incident)

1933	August - Appointed Lieutenant Colonel, Cavalry October - Finishes tour of duty and returns home via the Indian Ocean
	Attaché to the Division of Army Ministry's section of equestrian matters
	Lives in Shimokitazawa, Setagaya-ku, Tokyo
	1934 April - Decorated for merits regarding the Manchurian Incident (1931—34)
	Monetary award of 790
	September - Second daughter Takako is born
1936	August - moves to Asahikawa, Hokkaido, as Regiment Commander of the 7th Cavalry. Taro enrolls in Asahikawa Middle School
	(2.26 Incident)
1937	Appointed Colonel, Cavalry. Chief of section on equestrian matters
	Appointed committee member of army logistics
	September - Appointed Officer in Charge of equestrian matters
	(Sino-Japanese War erupts)
1938	Selects marching song for "Horse's Day"

1939   Moves to Yotsuya, Shinjuku-ku, Tokyo

Taro transfers to Seisoku Middle School

(Germany invades Poland, World War II erupts)

1940   March - Becomes Major General, attaché to the Narashino Second Cavalry Corps. Moves to Maatsubara-cho, Setagaya-ku, Tokyo

(Japan, Germany and Italy form alliance)

1941   Takako enters Matsubara Elementary School

October - Appointed Chief of Staff, South China Detail (the 23rd Army)

December - Chief of Staff of the siege of Hong Kong

December 28 - Participates in triumphant entry into Hong Kong

Returns to Guangdong to participate in tactical planning of the siege of Chungking

(Japan attacks Pearl Harbor, Pacific War starts)

1943   Receives decoration - Order of the Sacred Treasure, Gold and Silver Star

June - Made Lieutenant General and appointed as Commander of 2nd Guard Corps. Moves to official residence in Roppongi

1944   April - Assigned to Eastern Headquarters

Taro enters Waseda University, Science and Technology Dept.

May - Appointed Commander of the 109th Corps

June 10 - Leaves family for Iwo Jima. Takako is evacuated to the home of maternal grandparents in Sarashina-gun, Nagano Prefecture

July 1 - Appointed Commander of the entire Ogasawara Corps, reporting directly to Imperial Headquarters

(Fall of Saipan)

1945   February 19 - American military starts invasion of Iwo Jima

March 1 - Lieutenant General Kuribayashi's appointment as Supreme Commander of Ogasawara Area Corps is announced

March 16 - Date of last cable from Iwo Jima

March 17 - Japanese army makes final stand against the Americans

Kuribayashi is made full General of the army

March 26 - 54 years old, Kuribayashi dies in action

May 25 - Kuribayashi residence in Matsubara-cho,

Setagaya-ku is burned in air raid

(Great Tokyo Air Raid)

June - Yoshii and Yoko evacuate to Yamanashi Prefecture

August - Yoshii contracts typhoid fever and is hospitalized

(Defeat of Japan)

Yoshii's mother and daughter, Yoko, nurse Yoshii back to health, but the mother and Yoko die from typhoid fever

October - Yoshii and Takako reunite at Yoshii's father's home

1967	Tadamichi Kuribayashi is decorated by the government

Afterword

By Iris Yamashita (screenwriter)

Oftentimes, the springboard for a historical movie is a real-life character, whose story or first person account gives us a unique perspective into a time or place that might otherwise remain intangible. Considering World War II alone, we had such compelling movies as *Schindler's List*, based on the life of German industrialist Oskar Schindler, *Saving Private Ryan,* inspired by the true story of the Niland Brothers, and *Patton*, which revolved around America's most famous general. For *Letters from Iwo Jima,* it was Tadamichi Kuribayashi, the leading commander of the Japanese forces at one of the bloodiest battles of World War II, that became the inspiration for the movie.

Reading *Picture Letters from the Commander in Chief*, I was immediately struck by how different I imagined such a man of this renown would be. It was clear that Kuribayashi was a doting father, a talented caricature artist, a poet and a proper gentleman. He also showed a charming sense of humor through his numerous sketches which put himself as the object of derision—whether it was being mortified at a dance, taking a snooze on a chair, or doing stretching and bending exercises.

This, I believed, was the key to the film, to realize that many of the men of the Imperial Army might not have been so different from people we know. They were real people who had families and personalities and complexities that we could all identify with, placed in a situation of horror and chaos.

General Kuribayashi's inner conflicts became palpable. I could begin to imagine how he must have felt on the island, having once attended grand dinner parties with the men who were now on the other side of the line. "The United States is the last country in the world Japan should fight," he once wrote to his wife. On top of that, he had witnessed America's advances in technology firsthand. When his maid showed him her new car, he wrote, "This old woman's car looks better than the buses running around in the Japanese countryside. Japan has to do something about that." He was aware that his forces on the island would not only be outnumbered, but outmachined as well. "I fear that my chances for survival are less than one percent," he had written in one of his first letters home from Iwo Jima.

Above all, what resonated in these letters was the feeling of being homesick and lonely without his family. When Kuribayashi takes his final journey in the movie, it's that sense of loneliness, driving along an empty stretch of road that came to mind, wishing he could be with his family.

Ultimately, I felt the many nuances of Tadamichi Kuribayashi came to life on screen under Clint Eastwood's masterful direction and actor Ken Watanabe's deft portrayal, expressing the perfect sense of balance of the gentleness and warmth of a family man, combined with the strength, practicality and regality of a commanding officer.

Iris Yamashita is a screenwriter who was nominated for an Academy Award® along with co-story writer Paul Haggis for the movie, *Letters from Iwo Jima.*